ERICA GLESSING, Ed.

Sell Your House *Fast*
FOR THE
Right Price!

Successful Agents Share Tips on Mindset,
Pricing, Promoting, and Selling for Top Dollar

H   PY
PUBLISHING
an imprint of Wyatt-MacKenzie

Sell Your House Fast for the Right Price!
Compiled and Edited by Erica Glessing

F I R S T   E D I T I O N
ISBN: 978-1-936214-93-8
Library of Congress Control Number: 2012911946

Proofread by Salle Hayden, www.UpstartServices.com

REALTOR® is the registered trademark of the **National Association of REALTORS®**

Published by Happy Publishing, an imprint of Wyatt-MacKenzie
HappyPublishing@gmail.com

H   P   Y
P U B L I S H I N G
an imprint of Wyatt-MacKenzie

Dear Reader,

Last winter my heart fell when I looked at the equity of the two homes I own. A foreclosed home in bad condition on a nice lot sold for $225,000 a few houses from the house I own with my brother in a beautiful area of Marin County, California, just blocks from the beach. This took the value of my home down from its $750,000 value a few years back, and I felt forlorn and depressed.

Simultaneously, the home I live in plummeted from $725,000 to $450,000 and we owe $430,000. Without doing anything specifically to hurt the value of my homes, I lost several hundred thousand dollars! I decided right at that moment that if it was the right time to sell, I would do what it takes so that my own home sales would go smoothly. I decided that I wanted to call upon the brightest minds in the country to shed light on homes that sold fast, easily and without drama for the best price possible. I sought agents who do all the right things right. I set out to share stories of agent authors who line up home sales like dominoes so they flow and work and help the sellers with dignity, even when equity has changed and the market climate is unpredictable.

One of the first rock stars I signed was Albert Garibaldi, an Intero top tier agent in Northern California who is a gifted communicator, storyteller, and brilliant negotiator for his clients. Soon after Albert Garibaldi agreed to tell his success stories in this book, Barbara Hensley from Rockwall, Texas joined me. Barbara has sold more than 3,500 homes in her career. She brings class, energy, enthusiasm and experience to the repertoire of stories authors share in this book.

Each and every author was chosen carefully. The result? *Sell Your House Fast for the Right Price.* This book is brimming with more than two dozen stories of successful home sales in 15+ markets that span the United States. What emerges is a clear picture of how to sell a house that encompasses strategies for:

- Maintaining the best state of mind

- Losing resistance to the market

- Choosing your wall colors, navigating design elements for the best sale

- Knowing when to remove a wall

- Masking loud neighborhood noise

- Setting the price in a seductive fashion

- Marketing with the new bells, whistles and social media insight these stellar agents bring to the table.

Featured in this book are stories from 20 licensed real estate agents (including myself) who have sold more than 11,500 homes in our collective careers. That is a lot of talent, expertise and experience in one book. I am blessed to compile these stories for you. In the background, business coach and talented real estate magnate Michael Stott (one of the authors) was supporting the manuscript every step of the way.

May these stories be the grease, the glue, the insight, the foundation for you to stand on when you get ready to sell a house, or help a client sell a house. It's a lot easier than you thought it would be.

Sincerely,

Erica

Erica Glessing
CEO, Happy Publishing
Editor *Sell Your House Fast for the Right Price*

I. MINDSET...

II. PREPARING THE HOUSE FOR SALE...

MINDSET...

Hi Cora,

Passion Rules!

2013

CHAPTER 1

Passion, Strategy and Price Rule!

By Albert Garibaldi

Making the Right Move

It is an early spring evening and I am driving up to a home in Dublin that feeds to excellent schools. It has been sitting on the market for four months with another agent. I am meeting the owners for the first time.

The dad wants to move to a better high school enrollment area about 12 miles from this home. He has five children, and he is highly motivated. When we meet, I can feel their motivation. I can feel how intensely he wants to move, and the whole family is in agreement with this.

As I am walking through the house, I love the floor plan. It's got a great flow. I look for location, floor plan, and how well the house has been remodeled. I know when the location and flow are good, the buyer will be happy.

This home has it all! It has a great floor plan, with a full bathroom and bedroom downstairs, and the family room is in clear view from the kitchen. Everything works.

We look at the pricing together, and the previous agent priced this home about $100,000 over what homes like this are selling for in Dublin. We place the price at $835,000. Pricing a home right is about 95 percent of the marketing. Once you price it right, the home will bring in the buyer.

When we meet and go over the homes that have sold, the owner can see what is going on. It can be a challenge to see what is going on when you are focused on what you need for your next move. I work with this owner to see the sold home prices, and he decides to lower the price to make the home very enticing to possible buyers.

Within a few days, four offers come in and the home is sold for $850,000. In this situation, I'm helping the family buy a new home where they want to go in Danville CA. I negotiate for $80,000 in upgrades on the new home purchase.

The dad, sadly won't live two more years. But when he passes, he knows that his children will all be attending schools that are among the best in the state.

When I am meeting with people I feel so passionate about helping them get the home sold. I really care. I believe this carries into everything I do. I wanted to help this family move into a new home, and everything went smoothly during the process.

A Beautiful Home that Has Seen Better Days

When I was given the opportunity to sell a 5,000 square-foot home in Dublin Ranch, the very most expensive neighborhood of Dublin, California, I was excited about the opportunity. This is a bank owned home, though, and the previous owners trashed the interior. It is a complete disaster! The owners ripped out the railing, took all of the appliances, took the hardwood floors and even took the kitchen sink.

I'm looking around this neighborhood that is an absolute 10. The home feeds to excellent schools. And yet, the inside is a complete mess.

To replace appliances in this neighborhood, you have to select the most expensive appliances. I estimate the value around $150,000 to put everything back to rights. I had to make decisions about what was going to be repaired, and what could be left for the new owner to replace themselves.

I decided to put in a high end stove, and a new sink. I left out the dishwasher, fridge and oven for the new owners to replace themselves. I replaced carpet and painted. For safety, I replace the railings in the home. The repairs ran about $50,000 but we held off on another $100,000 in replacements and repairs. The bank (owner) was asking if we should replace the cabinets. My feeling was that this home had great schools, a great view, a fabulous neighborhood, and an excellent flow and floor plan. We decided to let the new owners choose their own appliances and price the home less than homes that were not selling in the area.

The homes that were not selling were priced around $1,300,000 to $1,400,000. We priced this home at $1,099,000 and sold it for $1,066,000 within 14 days.

I help people who are selling their homes to let go of being attached to the home they want to sell. Once you have less emotional attachment to the property, you are going to save yourself thousands of dollars. This is a point I feel strongly about. This process of feeling passionately about excellence, but not being attached to the outcome will help guide you to the strongest results.

The market is going to bring the best offer to your house when you move out of the way. Let the home be shown without you inside of it! Let the home be clear of your things. Clutter doesn't help you. Polish and brighten and clean and clear, but let the home shine on its own. This is hard to convey. When you are not attached, you're going to let the new owner get emotionally attached to the house. This will work in your favor.

When to Move a Wall

I walk into a foreclosed home a large national bank has hired me to sell. The flooring is old, the paint is chipped, and the rooms are dark. It is not in a great location, and the schools are not terrific.

What I'm thinking as I am walking through the house is that the flow is very choppy. The rooms are dark and gloomy. The kitchen doesn't really work. It needs some upgrades, especially because it is not in a great location. So I want the inside to be the best it can be.

I needed to upgrade the house with paint, carpet, and I brought in a construction company to remove a few walls. It is not that expensive to take out a wall, surprisingly. I wanted to give the buyer a remodeled look and feel, and a better flow. I opened up the kitchen, one of the most important rooms in selling a house.

I listed the home, in Danville, California for $719,000 and sold it for $740,000. We received four offers within a few days. The opening up of the kitchen and the inside of the home, plus brightening up with new paint and carpet, made for an easy sale in the end.

Every Day on Market is Precious

My philosophy about days on market is very strong. The bottom line is that you cannot allow your property to accumulate days on the market. When you accumulate days on market, you are going to lose leverage in your negotiations.

As I am driving up to see a home for the first time, I'm ranking everything on a scale of one to 10. I'm looking at the neighborhood, the street, the schools, and the condition of the house. Then once I'm inside the house,

I'm looking at the floor plan, the flow, and the remodeling inside the house.

I work with the home owner to price aggressively so that every day on the market is valuable.

One of the guiding factors that will go into the price a buyer will pay for your house will be the number of days on the market. If the home is not on the market long, it will receive higher offers than if it sits for months and months. I look carefully at responses in what I call "real time." I look for what happens the first few days? Within about a week, my phone should be ringing a lot if we have put the right price on a home. It should be sold within 21 days.

Staging Isn't Always the Answer

I was invited to meet with a family who owned a beautiful home that had been on the market for six months, with no offers. This home was staged for thousands of dollars, and sat still.

As I walk in, I can see the house is absolutely great. It's in a great place, about a mile from downtown Campbell, CA. The house has an excellent floor plan. I am thinking that the seller doesn't need to stage it at all. This is a brand new house. I am not against staging, but in some cases, when the home is beautifully remodeled or new, staging isn't always the answer.

In reality, the home was overpriced by about $100,000. I sat down with the seller and we looked at the homes that had recently sold in the same general size and quality. We priced the home at $1.35 million, down from $1.46 million. We received three offers within seven days.

One of the keys to figuring out the right price is to stay unattached. This is hard for the person selling the house, I can see that. When you look at the numbers objectively, you can figure out the price that will move and sell the house quickly.

In this case in Campbell, California, we took out the staging and let the home sell with a clear and uncluttered feeling. Plus, when we dropped the price, we opened up the house to new pools of buyers that would not see the home at the previous price.

The First Week on Market

What I should see in the first seven days is a lot of showings, a lot of phone calls from buyer agents, and a lot of feedback from the people who visit the home. The first seven days is so important.

Within two or three days, if a home is priced and prepared well, I should see interest. The activity at the open houses will also tell me a lot about how well it will sell. If I am not seeing a lot of activity within the first 14 days, it is time to re-evaluate the price and preparation of the house.

Here is the bottom line: you cannot allow your property to be on the market and accumulate more and more days on market. You lose all of your leverage to negotiate.

The Educated Buyer

I'm always looking for an offer from an educated buyer who understands what homes are worth. An educated buyer is someone who has seen 15 to 25 houses and who may have already offered too low and failed. A buyer who is not educated will be tempted to turn in a really low offer. If a buyer knows the market, they will make a good offer right away if the home is priced and prepared right.

What a Buyer Wants in their New Home

If the home has location and flow, I'm not going to worry as much about staging, interior and upgrades. If a home is in a poor location, or has a bad flow, a crunched or dark feeling inside, I'm going to know more has to be done inside to get the home sold.

A buyer wants location first, floor plan or flow second, and the interior upgrades third. If a home has a top ranked location and a great flow, the home will get a great market price regardless of the upgrades. If a home suffers in location or has some issues with floor plan, it is going to need remodeling or upgrades to sell for a good price.

The Motivated Home Seller

When I first meet with a person who wants to sell his or her home, I am looking at the motivation. I only want to work with people who are motivated in the eight, nine or 10 out of 10 range. If someone says "I would like to sell in a year or so," I'm going to wait and work with them when they are ready.

When I work with a home owner who is completely focused and motivated to sell, we are going to work together beautifully. I can tell this right away.

A Beautiful Location

I had the opportunity to sell a home in the lovely community of Los Altos, CA. The home was well-loved but never remodeled. Because this home is located in Los Altos, it is worth over $1 million on land value and location alone.

The owner has to make a decision. Does she put $100,000 into the home and worry about remodeling the house with new carpet, kitchen countertops, paint and significant repairs, or should she let the new buyer make the remodeling decisions? For this homeowner, the process of working on remodeling the family's home use seemed daunting. Plus, how could she be certain the new owner wouldn't want to make their own decisions?

She decided to list the home for a reasonable price (in Los Altos CA this translated to $1,199,000). We sold it less than a month at the asking price. The new buyers ended up building a nearly new home on the property. We saved the family a lot of time and energy.

I bring so much energy, passion and enthusiasm to every home I sell. I am motivated to help people, and I feel so strongly about keeping their best interest at heart. I believe this has something to do with the success I have been able to experience in my real estate career.

I believe that when I bring honesty, passion and enthusiasm to the situation, I am always going to help my clients get the most for their home, and sell their home in as short a time as possible for the best price possible. The best home sales happen when you combine excellent preparation, excellent service, and excellent marketing with excellent price setting. It is a great feeling to help my clients move on.

I follow these steps in selling a home, and this has served me well.

Aggressive pricing – I believe that pricing the home correctly is 95 percent of the marketing. Choose a price that will help bring offers right away.

Aggressive preparation – I am not afraid to move walls, get the home painted, upgrade with appliances, or make other changes that will help the home be seen in its best light. A home should be as outstanding as it can possibly be given its location, condition and market value.

Aggressive service – I treat each person as though each client is the only client I am serving. I want every buyer's agent to hear from me, and I want every one of my clients to know that I am here for them. I may not send long emails, but I always acknowledge an email. I like this responsiveness, and I know that people like this from me. It goes along with a standard of excellence I maintain in all of my business dealings.

Aggressive results – I know that I will receive excellent results. I am so confident in these results, because I know that if the client prepares the home well and we set it up right, the home will sell quickly and my clients can move. It is such a good feeling at this point in my career to provide excellent results. I love this. Nothing makes me happier than great results, regardless of the market trends. This is what I bring, and this is what I stand for.

ABOUT THE AUTHOR – *Albert Garibaldi*

Albert Garibaldi overcame learning disabilities to become one of the top real estate agents in the Silicon Valley, California region. He is driven by a desire to succeed, and a passion to do what is right for his clients.

Albert can remember how he first chose real estate as a career. About a decade ago, he was introduced to Gino Blefari, who was starting a company called Intero. They met for coffee and a conversation about real estate in California. Albert was inspired. He joined Intero, then grew to become one of the top one percent of the company that has grown to more than 2,000 agents worldwide.

Albert believes his learning disabilities actually strengthened his drive and passion to succeed. Because school was so difficult, he had to work harder than any other child to do reasonably well. He believes that this work ethic, strongly ingrained in his family and heritage, has served him well. When he first started at Intero, he would drive to one of the founder's homes at 5 a.m. daily for a workout session and personalized real estate coaching. Over weight lifting, the two would talk about Albert's progress and focus Albert's energy where he could most succeed.

Every few weeks now, Albert takes his real estate expertise into the classroom and instructs newer agents at his company on best practices. He believes in giving back to the company that has supported his meteoric rise so well.

Albert brings attention to detail and resourcefulness to each and every one of his clients. Albert's clients always feel like he is looking out for their best interest. He responds quickly to their voice mails and emails, even when he is managing a large portfolio of homes for sale.

With the goal of creating relationships for life, Albert works through every detail of the home buying and selling process with his clients, making them feel safe, secure and well represented. His ability to genuinely listen to a client's needs enables Albert to immediately focus in and achieve results. With over 20 years of sales industry experience, Albert has built a thriving team oriented real estate business.

Albert's work ethic is a result of his comprehensive understanding of a real estate transaction. Albert's insight is a unique blend of big picture strategy and daily details. With over 500 homes sold in less than 14 years, he is on track. To bring balance to his hard-working life, Albert has several hobbies. His interests include physical fitness, the outdoors, and spending time with his wife, Deanna and their three children, Dominic, Nicolino and Daniella. Email Albert at AGaribaldi@interorealestate.com.

CHAPTER 2

Smooth Sailing for Southwest Florida Home Sales

By A.J. Ackerman

David and Denise: Moving Up

I received a call from a couple named David and Denise. They were builders, and owned a gorgeous home on the water in Cape Coral that had direct access to the Gulf of Mexico. Although they loved the house, they decided it was time to sell it and build a larger home that better fit their needs.

The couple called after receiving a "Just Sold" postcard and recommendation letter from a neighbor who's home I had just sold. After meeting with David and Denise, I could sense that they were excited about the opportunity to sell their house, and embark on the new adventure of building a larger home. We met at the house, and I could tell within an instant that it would be easy to sell. The house was absolutely immaculate! Because they were custom builders from up North, the house had a special feel to it, with unique characteristics that you typically wouldn't find in a lot of homes in Florida.

The home contained gorgeous, rich cherry wood, beautiful tile, and a huge kitchen with granite countertops. Looking through the sliding glass doors, I took in the view of a beautiful pool and jacuzzi in a giant lanai, with the glistening water and boat dock just beyond the pool. I felt like I was in a model home. I knew that once a new couple or family stepped into the beautiful corridors of the home, experienced the breathtaking view of the water, and felt the breezes flowing through the house, they would easily fall in love with it!

I reviewed strategies with David and Denise, and we discussed a price that I thought would work. They actually wanted to go lower, but I convinced them that this beautiful home would easily sell for a higher price. I scheduled an open house and set up a virtual tour on my website. From the first open house, we had a buyer, and sold the home in only six days! Within 30 days, the home was sold (escrow closed), and the couple was happily on their way to building a new, larger home.

David and Denise expressed how much they appreciated my passion for real estate and the straightforward ideas to get them top dollar for the home.

I recommend the "Just Sold" letter to any agents who are seeking to grow their business. The "Just Sold" letter is something that I send out to other homeowners in a neighborhood when I've sold one of their neighbors' homes. This tells people that homes in their neighborhood are selling, and provides information in case they, or anyone they know, may also be thinking about selling their home. It's a great way to provide people with inspiration about the real estate market, and motivation to sell their house!

Tom and Carol's Home: An Easy Short Sale

Tom and Carol called me after receiving a postcard I'd sent which offered them a free report on house prices in their location of Cape Coral. It allowed them to see what comparable houses were selling for, and was the motivation they needed to make the decision to sell their home. After talking to them on the phone, I could tell they were genuinely nice people. They were in a difficult financial situation and absolutely needed to sell their home. However, they owed more on it than what comparable houses were selling for in their area. This meant that a short sale was needed. They were very nervous about doing a short sale, because their only knowledge of it was based on what they had heard from the media. Once I explained the process, and told them what to expect, they began to feel more at ease about it, and they were ready to move forward. A short sale means that the mortgage owed exceeds the current market value of the home, and the bank will have to forgive a portion of the debt for the home to be sold.

When I met them at their house, I was excited about getting started. It was a beautiful home with a pool in Southwest Cape Coral. The location was absolutely impeccable! It had an amazing floor plan, and was a newer home with high ceilings and beautiful tile. The house was right on the water, with access to the Gulf. I told them the price they could expect, and they actually didn't even believe me at first.

The price we set worked. We had the first buyer in a contract to purchase the home within two weeks of putting it up for sale. Although the first contract fell through, we received another offer two days later, and then the home was sold. It took about three months for the short sale process to conclude. This was very normal. Tom and Carol were pleasantly surprised that we were able to get through the short sale process and sell their house so quickly, and without any of the complications they dreaded. This was a situation in which they expected the worst and the sale went smoothly and right on track.

The couple appreciated the time I spent helping them understand the short sale process; dealing with their attorney; and making sure everything went smoothly. Tom said that, "In the six real estate transactions I have had, this was the most complex and at the same time the easiest process ever due to your efforts."

It's always a great feeling to walk away from a home sale where everyone feels like they've won. So many people are worried that a short sale will drag out, and become an arduous, unpleasant experience. I feel that selling your home should be a fun and exciting adventure! It's an opportunity to move onto the next stage of your life! Even through a short sale process, my goal is to make sure that the seller still feels that same sense of excitement and ease.

John's Home Sale: Moving Quickly

From our first conversation, I could tell that John was a really nice guy. It was obvious that he sincerely loved his home, and had put a lot of time into making it a truly amazing place to live. But, he was at a point in his life where he was looking for a new start, and the first step was selling his current home.

When I met with John at his house, I was very impressed with how beautifully decorated it was. He had made the most of a great layout. It was about 2400 square feet, located on a corner lot. It also had a 3-car garage, pool, and jacuzzi. Walking through the home, it felt warm and comfortable. He'd added some cool little details, like a rainfall shower with jets, and planters in all the bedrooms.

John was focused on a goal of a getting a certain price for the house. He felt it was important to sell it at that number or higher. However, he was also very concerned with selling it quickly, due to his financial situation. I shared with him the price that I felt was realistic, in order to sell it within his time frame. The numbers did not agree, but he said that he was very impressed with the fact that I was straightforward from the beginning, and hired me to sell the home for a price we agreed would be right.

I scheduled an open house for a few weeks after we listed the home. The buyer who would ultimately purchase the home attended the open house, and thought it would be a strong investment property that they could easily rent out. In only two weeks after the open house, they made the decision to buy the house. John was also looking to sell the furniture, and I was even able to sell all of it for him!

John's original goal was to have the home sold in 90 days. We actually closed escrow in less than 60 days, at a price that allowed him to pay off the loan and even have an extra $10,000 in his pocket. Needless to say, John was extremely happy!

Barbara's Home Sale: Time to Downsize!

Barbara is a wonderful lady. She's in her 80s, but you would never know it by the way she acts. She knows what she wants, loves to work on her house, and is very independent. Barbara was recently widowed when her husband was tragically hit by a car. It had been two years since her husband passed, so Barbara decided it was time to downsize into a smaller home. That's when she called.

Barbara decided to call me because she'd come across me a lot on the internet. She had also received a postcard that I sent out which was offering a free report about home values in her area. I stayed in contact with her for six months after the first time she called. She decided to call me when she was actually ready to sell her home.

The home she was living in was simply beautiful. It was a "Dream Villa" built home on a canal with Gulf access, located in a prime spot in Southwest Cape Coral. The landscaping was pristine, and the house featured a huge dock with a little Tiki Hut and a 13,000-pound boat lift. The house had new carpet, 12-feet-high vaulted ceilings, and a lighted tray ceiling in the master bedroom. It also had surround sound throughout the house. Barbara loved her house, but it was a lot more than she needed living by herself.

I suggested a price that I thought would sell her home in about 90 days. We priced it a little high. She had high expectations. I suggested to her that she should purchase a one-year home warranty, because her air conditioning was very old, and could end up costing her money if it needed repairs before the close of the home sale. She took this advice, and was so glad she did! The air conditioner completely went out before the home sold, and it would have ended up costing her $2,500 to repair!

We had a few open houses in the very first three weeks, and after the third open house, the home sold! The home sold so quickly that she was still in the process of having her new, smaller home built. We worked out a delay at closing to give her time to complete it. It actually worked out for the best, because this also allowed the buyers from up North the flexibility to take their time moving down.

Once Barbara's new home was finished, I helped her move (even though she insisted she could do it on her own!) The whole process was such a rewarding experience, and reminded me, yet again, why I truly love what I do.

ABOUT THE AUTHOR – *A.J. Ackerman*

A.J. Ackerman loves working in real estate, and his true passion lies in helping people. He finds fulfillment in both his professional and personal life by helping others make a positive change in their lives. A.J. uses his experience and knowledge about real estate to reach this goal.

To A.J., "real estate" is much more than the transaction of buying or selling a house, it is about helping a person transition into a new stage of life. His goal is to help others envision the life which they desire, understand what makes them happy, and help them reach this point. Often, this can involve a change in a person's location, environment, or surroundings. Maybe it's about moving into a larger home to start a family, or maybe it's about simplifying and relocating to enjoy a new lifestyle in retirement. Perhaps it's just about making a fresh start in life, beginning with a change in your living environment.

A.J. believes in building relationships. He maintains a deep seeded understanding that helping others breeds long term happiness and success in his own life. Therefore, A.J. puts his heart and his full dedication into every one of his real estate transactions. His vision for a person, for a community, and for long term happiness is evident in every interaction that he has. It is because of this genuine passion and understanding, combined with extensive experience and knowledge, that A.J. has become such a success in his field. He also attributes this success to the very experienced team of full-time professionals that he has chosen to work with.

The stories shared in this book are only a small sampling of the clients who can attest to A.J.'s dedication to helping people, not only through the process of buying or selling their home, but through the transition of a new beginning in their life.

For more information about A.J. Ackerman & Associates, call 239-565-7867 or visit www.ackermanswfl.com.

CHAPTER 3

The Bittersweet Sale: Selling the Family Homestead

By Mal Duane

Over the past several years I have experienced an increase in working with elderly clients or their heirs to sell "the family homestead." The homestead is generally a house that has been lived in for decades, and has served, not only as a residence, but also as a monument to the entire family. Because of the emotional and financial components involved, the sale of the family homestead requires a great deal of preparation, compassion and patience. The amount of time between our first introduction and the property hitting the market can typically last several months. Through my experience, I have developed a proven, successful plan to take everything through the evaluation and selling process to a smooth closing. Whether you're an agent, or a seller, this is not a quick process but can ultimately result in a very timely sale if you keep the following in mind:

Exercise Patience: Remember to remain calm and patient throughout the process. This is especially true for agents when dealing with elderly owners or their heirs. This is an emotional process.

Gather Paperwork: Pull together utility bills for the past two years, a current tax bill and a copy of the deed and plot plan.

Anticipate: Make sure there are no unknown financial surprises before the closing, including unpaid taxes or bills.

Evaluate and Remove Possessions: Whether you are an agent, or a seller, hire a professional company to perform this task, as emotions are taken out of the process. Continue until the house is empty. If property needs staging, this can be done after the owner's contents are removed.

Prioritize and Repair: Make an assessment of all repairs needed and then prioritize them. Safety issues are mandatory. Also there may be new building code requirements that have to be updated regarding smoke detectors or lines to oil tanks.

Clean: Get the house as clean as possible, inside and out. Although it may be old, cleanliness is a must.

Price: Keep in mind the future potential that exists in the property, but also create a fair price, so the buyers find good value.

Inform: It is imperative to keep all parties, attorney, owner or heirs notified of your progress.

In our current environment, I realize that a "smooth closing" is a bit unusual, so let me share with you two examples, one where the owner was present and the other where the heirs were selling the property. In both examples, I adhere to the 8-step plan above.

Wyatt: The Owner

Just a few days shy of turning 90 years old, Wyatt pulled up to the property in a shiny Buick that was as long as his driveway. Expecting an elderly man, I was quite surprised when a perky fellow practically jumped out of the Buick with a manila folder in hand. He shook my hand, then proceeded to tell me that everything I need to get started should be contained in the folder.

I accepted the folder from him and began to read through it. Inside the folder was **all the key paperwork necessary to sell the property**:

· A neatly typed list of all improvements he had made over the 50-year window of his ownership

· All of his utility bills for the past two years

· A current tax bill

· A copy of his deed and plot plan

I was astounded at his level of preparedness but soon learned he was an attorney.

As we toured his home, he started to describe how he

lived there with his precious Kate who had passed a few years before. I could almost envision his family in the home. His eyes lit up as he spoke. He gave a complete history of the neighborhood, which was fascinating. Wyatt was now residing in assisted living — the new breed of residential living for the elderly. He wasn't happy about being there, but relinquished that it was probably for the best.

The house was empty of all personal content. Again, Wyatt was prepared to sell his home. This is not usually the case. It usually takes an average of three months to organize the owners' contents.. I work with a professional company called "It's Your Move". They inventory everything in the house with the owner. They are so skillful at making suggestions on what they should take and what they should "donate". The word thrown out is never spoken. Elderly people can be very protective of their belongings. It takes patience and compassion to sort through all of this and whittle it down to what will now probably fit into a smaller living space.

After two hours of measuring and taking photos, Wyatt and I decided on a listing date. The house was well maintained and I did not see any blaring deferred maintenance, which would need to be dealt with before putting the property on the market. I suggested a power washing outside to freshen up the clapboards and we would be ready to go.

He had realistic expectations as to the value. When I presented the market analysis, he was receptive to my pricing suggestions. **Because Wyatt had done his**

homework, had all the necessary documentation needed and got the home empty and clean, his family homestead sold in 14 days for almost asking price.

We scheduled the closing and the final walk through. Wyatt wanted to meet the buyers and show them everything they needed to know about the operations of the house. I know the buyer was so touched by all his help. As we exited the home for the final time, he turned and looked back inside one more time and I noticed his eyes fill up with tears. He was closing the book on the best chapters of his life. I had to bite my lip not to cry myself. It is a very emotional experience for an elderly person to let go of their "castle". We need to remember how huge a change this is. My friendship continued long after the closing. We would connect once or twice a year, I would drop buy and visit him at his assisted living residence and bring maple walnut ice cream, his favorite. We would talk about the Red Sox or the Patriots but we never mentioned the house again.

On the flip side of the sale of Wyatt's home, I will share how things work with an estate sale where there has never been any preparation made. Often times, folks decide they want to live their life out where they are. The heirs are left with a property that can be run down and filled to the brim with "stuff". This type of sale can take several months of planning and legal work to establish the executor of the estate. In addition to the **paperwork** necessary to sell the home, permission to sell must be acquired before the estate property can be legally sold.

Next, a professional company can be hired to **evaluate the contents of the home and organize/remove them**. Once the house is empty, schedule the necessary contractors to perform the **repairs** that are really required to get the home sold. All safety, some cosmetic and pest treatments should be completed before going on the market. The amount of work that is done is really predicated on the financial status of the estate. If there is money available, focus repairs on priority items only.

The estate sale can be complex because there may be three or four different heirs, who may not be in agreement with the action steps they should take. If you're an agent, **inform** the heirs of your intended action plan, giving as much detailed information as possible. For example, if the interior of the home requires updates, explain why **aggressive pricing** is usually the best strategy to sell the home.

If you're a seller, whether or not you hire an agent, remember there is always an element of emotional attachment to the home that creates value to the owners that a buyer or agent may not see. If you're the seller, you have to put your emotions aside when you consider pricing the estate, or put our emotions aside and follow the lead of the professional you hire. They are looking for the best location, condition and size for the price that they qualify for. In today's market, homes must meet several criteria before an offer is even considered. The competition is fierce and everyone is competing for those limited few who are able to get a mortgage.

And whether you are a seller or an agent, it is imperative to bring the best product forward in today's selling environment, even if it means spending a little more out of pocket to do so.

The Davis Family's Estate Sale

My client, the Davis family, had just put their grandfather's house on the market. It was an adorable vintage colonial with a fenced in yard in a nice neighborhood, but once inside, that impression changed quickly. There were water-stained ceilings, terribly worn hardwood floors and faded wallpaper peeling away from the walls. Many of the ceilings had severely cracked plaster, and I discovered the evidence of previous furry inhabitants all over the place. Obviously no home maintenance had occurred in years.

Since all the paperwork was in place, I immediately commenced with cleaning and repairing the home. It took a week with a professional crew to strip the wallpaper, paint all the walls beige, wash and polish the floors, patch the ceilings and perform a deep cleaning. They power-washed the outside of the home and cleaned all the windows, cut the grass and cleaned the yard of debris. It wasn't perfect but the potential came shining through.

The home was listed on a Monday at a price that reflected future improvements a new owner would want to do. By Friday, we had multiple offers all within two percent of the asking price or higher.

So, if you're going to sell the family homestead, get

prepared and remain informed. Do your homework and **get all your documents** organized. You need to work with a Realtor® who has the contacts and the expertise to get the home **cleaned**, **repaired**, and **ready** for sale. If you choose not to conduct repairs, keep these tips in mind and try to leave emotions out of the sale, especially when **pricing** the homestead. **Exercise patience**: this is not a quick process but can ultimately result in a very timely sale.

ABOUT THE AUTHOR – *Mal Duane*

Mal Duane, ABR, ASP, CRS, GRI, LTG, SRES, LMS and RECS has been selling homes for twenty-five years in her market area west of Boston, MA. She has continually been recognized over the years as a mega producing agent and leader in innovative internet marketing to get homes sold. Mal has been featured nationally in the CRS magazine, the National Real Estate Cyber Convention as well as speaking as a top producer in many national organizations. She knows how to get her clients top dollar in a down market.

Mal is also a bestselling author with a No. 1 book on Amazon.com titled <u>Alpha Chick: Five Steps for</u> <u>Moving from Pain to Power</u>. She is passionate about helping women recreate their lives and discover their life's purpose. A portion of all proceeds go to Holly's Gift an educational assistance fund that Mal started to help educate women in need.

You can reach Mal at her Keller Williams Metrowest Office, 12 Library Street, Framingham MA or email her at malduane@malduane.com.

CHAPTER 4

Price Is King! Location Rocks! Condition Closes! Timing Trumps All!

By Barbara Hensley

Selling your home fast for the right price is possible in any market. There is not one key factor, but several and they must all come into play in order to achieve this goal.

Price is king, but getting it right takes serious consideration of location and condition. If either or both of these factors are less than stellar, the price must be adjusted accordingly. This rule applies to all price ranges of homes, starter homes to luxury homes.

Timing trumps all! Never has timing been more important. Timing is fluid, changing constantly. What was
excellent timing yesterday can and will likely change
today. When the housing market bubble started
bursting a few years ago, most did not realize or expect
that it would impact the market so severely and for so
long, changing the real estate market forever.

My passion for marketing includes all types of homes
and price points, and I could share thousands of actual
stories about mistakes that have been made as well as
success stories. What follows is a cross-section of seller
experiences in getting their homes sold and the price
points range from less than $100,000 to almost
$3,000,000.

My Savvy Young First Time Home Seller Did Everything Right

I received a call from someone who was relocating to
another state. The home was his first home and he had
proudly taken good care of it during the several years
of being a home owner. Several years should have
brought a price increase to allow him to break out of
the property without losing any money. Right? Wrong!
I carefully worked on pricing and was disappointed to
tell him the news that no seller wants to hear. He would
have to bring money to the closing table to sell his
home, in the amount of several thousand dollars. He
had already moved out of the home, and would
continue making payments including taxes and insurance, as well as maintaining the yard and paying
utilities until the home sells.

There were other similar homes in the neighborhood priced more than my suggested price, but they had been on the market awhile and were not selling. ***This young seller listened and quickly grasped that each day the home is on the market would cost him money.***

As we talked, he considered the cost of keeping up his current home, meanwhile paying to live in the new location. He could not buy another home until he could sell this one. He quickly "got it" when I explained that the first two to three weeks would be when he would get the most activity and each week thereafter would attract lower offers, if any. He priced the home right. The home sold right away! An executed contract was worked in 10 days, meaning we could close before his next payment was due, stopping the outgoing flow of money.

This savvy young first-time seller did not beg the question "can we get more by waiting?" It was easy to do the math, resulting in a better long term bottom line for him. He was happily able to move to the next phase in his life. He was listed, contracted and closed while other homes in the neighborhood stayed on the market.

This young seller got it when many other sellers did not. He did everything right, including pricing and preparing the home to show to the best advantage. Joyfully it was sold to another first-time home buyer! The home was priced in the mid $130,000 range, a hot market in Texas IF the price is right, the condition good and the home is located in a good location. This one had it all!

Don't Follow the Market Down! The Story of Too Little, Too Late!

The flip side to the story of the savvy young first-time seller was a home placed on the market a couple of years before. At the list date, the home was priced right for the market. There were drastic changes going on in the real estate market with foreclosures and short sales, and the market value of homes in the area was decreasing rapidly.

These were motivated sellers but they were slow to reduce the price. I encouraged them to get ahead of the curve with a reduction which would bring a buyer. They were slow and behind the curve when they made their final reduction. I told them I felt we could get it sold quickly at the reduced price, and we did, almost immediately.

These sellers actually had to take money to close on their home. Had they changed the price earlier – rather than following the market down – they could have brought money home. The delay cost them dearly, each day adding more to the ultimate loss. It was a bittersweet closing. It was all about timing.

Welcome Back, Mr. and Mrs. Seller!

I had the opportunity to list an older home in an established neighborhood and we priced it at a good price at the time. The market quickly headed downward, but the sellers, who had lived in the home for 30 years, were focused on a certain price for the home. The sellers didn't want to consider the current comparative sales information. They were concerned with what they wanted for their home. They were certain it had features other homes in the area did not have. These features, however, were special only to the sellers and did not impact the market value of the house.

I explained that the longer it remained on the market, the less the final selling price would be. They had already purchased and moved into a new home. This home was vacant and even though there was not a mortgage payment they would continue to pay taxes, insurance, utilities and yard maintenance on the empty home. This home was now a money pit. Showings slowed down and there were no offers. They remained stuck on the price they wanted, as opposed to the price it would sell in the current market.

It was time for me to release this listing and encourage them to find someone one else to market the home at their price rather than actual market price. I wished them good luck.

About four months later I received a call. The sellers wanted to come back home – to me! They missed my marketing. They missed being able to reach their agent easily. They listened to my pricing advice this time and priced it at the magic number. The new price resulted in numerous showings and an executed contract. The cost of the delay was expensive, but the home ultimately sold.

Wedding Bells Would Soon Be Ringing for This Seller!

The sound of wedding bells was luring this widowed

homeowner away from the huge home custom built many years ago for his young family. The children had now moved on and it was time to sell the home. Plus he was hearing those distant wedding bells and doors opening to a new life in another state.

Was this great motivation? Yes, he wanted a quick sale, BUT he wanted to get top dollar for a home that had not been updated and reflected his "widowed" status. He found it difficult to see his memory filled home through the eyes of potential buyers. He was willing to keep an open-mind, but I could see that it would be a process to get the home priced to sell fast.

I immediately knew the neighborhood was a **prime location** with gorgeous mature trees and lush landscaping. There were no new homes to compete with in neighborhood, but most of the homes had been updated. The floor plan was not great and did not flow well for the average family and the interior of the home would be a hard sell! A really hard sell! This home was dated! It is impossible to compare an updated home to one that has not been updated, unless the price properly reflects this.

Enter My Friend Sharon, the Stager, with Her Magic Wand

This seller did not want to spend much money and we knew we had a challenge. This was not a home to completely update, as it would be too costly, take valuable time and ultimately net less money. The floor plan could not be changed and there would be no major updating. Oh my!

Miracle-working Sharon waved her magic wand. Sharon performed lots of just plain grunt work and the place was quickly looking better. The colors throughout the home were rather faded, and were long-out-of-vogue country blue tones. Sharon installed upscale accessories including classic blue and white oriental pieces, plus a few lime green and red accents to provide a more upscale modern look. Many old pictures, nick-knacks, faded artificial flowers and furnishings were removed. The remaining furnishings were rearranged to provide a more open and spacious look to this traditional home.

The seller had taken out the carpet in the family room, hall and master bedroom and stained the bare concrete. This was concrete not meant for staining and every flaw showed. This type of flooring treatment did not blend well with the traditional style of the home. The most affordable solution was new carpet and the seller agreed. Careful shopping and my real estate professional discount resulted in an affordable fix and lots of bang for the buck.

We changed the things that could be changed, got rid of a bunch of the old tired furnishings and accessories, conducted major de-cluttering and purchased new carpet to cover the concrete floors. The seller watched as coffee makers, toasters, slow cookers and a lot of other stuff were removed from the counter tops. A couple of simple bowls of green pears and red apples were placed to add color. WOW! What a difference! The countertops and appliances still needed updating, but now you could see what a lot of cabinet and counter space this large kitchen had to offer. Was the house still dated? You bet, but now prospective buyers could see the potential of this spacious home.

Now to the final pricing decision! The seller, while disappointed at my suggested list price, agreed on a reasonable price and a plan for a quick reduction. The neighborhood had lured a number of showings, but no offers.

Feedback from showings confirmed that the floor plan was not popular and that the home was dated. No one was willing to offer on the initial list price for a home needing new appliances, new countertops, and more new floor coverings. I knew we could not waste any more precious days on the market.

It was time to ask the seller for that price reduction! The seller was realistic and agreed to a speedy reduction. The showings immediately increased and the home was sold! A good solid contract was executed quickly.

This is a prime example of getting the price right for the condition of the home. The location was already awesome and the new pricing attracted buyers wanting a large home in this neighborhood. Congratulations to the new homeowners who could now update the home and to the happy seller who could answer the call of the wedding bells and move on to new experiences.

Selling the Best Estate Home in the Area for the Price! Easy? Not Always!

I was elated to get the call to visit owners of one of the

most stunning estate properties in the area to discuss placing the property on the market. Everyone in the area knows and admires this huge home situated at the top of a hill overlooking 20 gorgeous acres behind an impressive electronic estate gate.

I was hopeful the owners would be realistic about pricing and was pleased when they agreed to a price that I felt was right for the home, a good value for the land and the glorious 10,000-plus square-foot home. The presentation, pricing and marketing immediately resulted in qualified showings. We had it right!

Price was right! Condition was excellent! Location was the best! The sellers always made the home available to show!

We received an offer right away from a buyer relocating to Texas from California. Forward to closing! Not so fast. Just two days away from the expiration of the option period, the buyer opted out. While he was in Texas going to contract on this home, things had changed, DRASTICALLY! The stock market took a huge dip and the buyer lost most of the money he planned to use to pay cash for his new Texas home.

We received another offer, also a California buyer, and we were ready to go forward again. Then Wall Street struck again! This buyer no longer had the money to go forward with the purchase.

Okay, the third time is the charm, right? Wrong again! The third buyer went on contract and was anxious to close. Money in place one day was gone the next.

Proof of this luxury estate being priced right at the time was all three of these contracts were for almost the same price. Price was not the issue! The issue emerged was the suddenly wild ride being experienced on Wall Street. Suddenly the luxury home market was drying up! Luxury home buyers no longer had access to the funds needed to close. Additionally, buyers from California and other states were not able to sell their homes or at least not at a price point allowing them to purchase the homes they longed to buy at incredible prices in Texas.

The motivated owners of this estate started aggressively dropping the price. Even at new price points there were no comparatively sold homes. There were none because the multi-million dollar homes were not selling. Huge price reductions did not bring buyers. There were no luxury home buyers in the market.

This property followed the market down, but not because the owner was not flexible and willing to reduce the price. It was because there were no buyers for luxury homes anywhere in the area.

The home finally sold and closed at about half of the original list price at a great loss. It was one of only three homes selling for over a million dollars for the entire year of 2011 for the county.

The buyer came from many states away to take advantage of what is likely the deal of the century. The buyer was working with a real estate professional from out of my area, looking for an estate property on acreage. He would be moving his family and company to the Dallas area. Superior global internet marketing promoted and supported the value and beauty of this property and this far away buyer realized the value and potential of this outstanding property.

Timing! It Is NOW All about Timing!

Getting the price right in the beginning is important. Staying on top of market changes and being flexible enough to stay ahead of the curve of a decreasing market is a must. It is important to know and understand the cost of keeping your home. You may be amazed at how much your home is costing you each day it remains on the market. This is money out of your bottom line when the home does sell. I believe in keeping my clients informed, always telling them the truth, even when it hurts. Educated sellers can make informed decisions.

Sometimes Cutting Your Losses Can Be a Big Win!

Sell Your House Fast for the Right Price can happen, but you must forget past selling experiences and be ready to be flexible, open minded and brave enough to fight the battle. Selling your home is not a sport, but a war, a battle to get the best buyer for your home at a specific time. The price you get today may be the highest price you will ever get. Each year your home is another year older, and must compete with newer homes or more recently updated homes.

There is a reason you wanted to sell your home in the first place, and, while you may be disappointed in the price it will sell for, you likely still have a strong desire to sell your home and move on to the next phase in your life perhaps relocating or down sizing.

Making educated decisions will result in being able to close one door and immediately open many new doors once you sell the home that no longer fits your needs. *This is not the time to be emotional, it is a time to be wise and brave accepting the "what is" and looking forward to the "what can be".*

Hiring the right Realtor® is the glue that holds everything together

Pricing, location, condition and timing are all top priorities but engaging the right Realtor® should be number one on the list! Expect your real estate professional to carefully guide you through the battlefield of selling your home AND to be a master at global marketing with today's latest methods and tools.

ABOUT THE AUTHOR – *Barbara Hensley*

A series of corporate relocations took me from my Texas home to Oklahoma, Kansas, California, and Illinois and back to my beloved Texas. I quickly became a master at interviewing movers, packing, settling children in schools, learning about our new home towns and getting involved in each community as we made our way across the nation.

While I loved Texas, I realized that I never lived in a place I did not like. A friend once told me "You just bloom wherever you are planted!" Oh, I experienced all the pains of leaving family and friends and moving my two daughters around the country with tears in their eyes as they waved goodbye. I carefully researched each new area to learn how our family would fit in our new hometown. I treated each new town as our hometown and we became part of it. My favorite saying to my family after each move was "We have to get out and about our new town". I became an expert on relocation without benefit of the Internet of today. It blows my mind to think what I could have done with Internet access!

Once planted back again in the Dallas area in Rockwall on Lake Ray Hubbard I quickly became involved in the community and we felt at home within weeks. Little did I realize these relocation experiences were preparing me for an unexpected new career. I soon became a licensed Texas Realtor® in my new hometown, Rockwall and the rest is history! I have always said that real estate just rained on me and an amazing unexpected new career blossomed taking deep root in MY hometown. I take great pride in having been recognized as "the lady who put Rockwall County on the map."

Blessed with an exuberant amount of energy, strong work ethics and an ever growing passion for marketing and all things real estate, combined with my love affair with my new hometown, Rockwall, I was launched full force into an unbelievable journey now covering over three decades. I felt like Dorothy must have felt landing in the Land of Oz!

What a journey this has been! Extensive marketing and branding resulted in my company having over 50% of the total market share for the area by the mid nineties.

I have been honored to serve on the Board of Directors for: Greater Dallas Association of Realtors® (now MetroTex), Texas Association of Realtors®, Rockwall YMCA, Affiliate Group of Home and Apartment Builders Association, Rockwall Noon Rotary Club, Fulton Academy Private School, Earl Campbell Foundation, Rockwall Chamber of Commerce, and the Advisory Board for American National Bank.

Honors most cherished are receiving the Realtor® of the Year/Easterwood Award from the Greater Dallas Association of Realtors®, Member of the Year from the Rockwall Chamber of Commerce, RE/MAX Hall of Fame and the recently created "Rockwall Icons" from MetroTex for this area. National awards for promotions, advertising, sales and relocation resulted in local, state and national recognition.

The Barbara Hensley Teen Board received vast area recognition as well as coverage in Realtor® Magazines. These popular young teen board members assisted relocating teens in becoming involved in their new schools and community. The Teen Board attracted relocating families seeking help to pave the way for a smoother relocation for their teens and resulted in many homes being sold.

It's all about showmanship! I don't apologize for my strong desire to be first, to be THE Realtor® with the latest cutting edge marketing, followed by others, while I was moving on to the next unique promotion. Strong work ethics and an innate sense of fairness and loyalty have resulted in life long clients and amazing referrals.

Contact me for my eBook for Sellers and My Quick Start Action Plan. barbara@barbarahensley.com 972-772-9699 www.BarbaraHensleySellsTexas.com www.BarbaraHensley.com

CHAPTER 5

Sell Your House Fast in a New York Minute

By Paul Macapagal

Sell Your House Fast with the Right Pricing

Recently I came across a really nice listing in the Upper West Side area of Manhattan. It was a renovated one-bedroom, one-bathroom with great city views and terrific sunlight. The owners, Chris and Carolina, were trying to sell their property as a For Sale By Owner (FSBO). I decided to call the owners to schedule an opportunity to preview the property. In my initial conversation with Chris, I was invited to come by his open house to meet him and his wife and to preview the property the following day. When I arrived at the property the next day I was expecting a little bit more of an intimate meeting with the owners, not 15 other agents looking at the property at the same time. To my surprise, the open house Chris had scheduled was just for agents. As you can imagine, my first time meeting the owners and being in a one-bedroom with 15 other agents was a little hectic. All the agents in the room were vying for the owner's attention. All I kept saying to myself at the time was "what did I get myself into?" I kept a level head and pretended that I was alone in the room.

Prior to meeting the owners, I did my homework on the property and checked the past sales in the building, as well as in the area. The owners were asking $699,000 for the property. Based on the current market conditions and past sales, I could not justify the property selling for that amount. My estimates were the property should trade between the prices of $540,000 to $560,000. Armed with knowledge of the property, the building, and the area, I was confident that I could answer any and all the questions they owners could throw at me.

While I was in the broker's open house, Chris was asking the agents in the room some basic questions about his property, like, "How do you like the property?" "What do you think of the renovations?" "What do you think of the building?" These were all the questions that all the other agents were so quick to answer. There was however, one question in particular that the owner asked and nobody seemed to have the guts to answer. That question was "so, what do you think of my price?" All the agents in the room started to look at each other. There was a very weird and empty silence that filled the room. I can understand why the silence took place. All of the agents knew the property was over-priced, but no one wanted to be the bearer of bad news. Since I had nothing to lose and no one stepped up to the plate, I decide to swing the bat and answer the question. I said with conviction, "Your property is over-priced based on the past sales in the area." I began talking about the direct competition currently on the market, and the value of the renovations that were put into the unit. And I even went as far as to say, "even if you got the full asking price for your property, a bank would not lend the money to the buyer because the property would not appraise at that amount. " He then asked me what I think it should be listed for and I said $550,000. I truly thought at that point the owner was going to ask me to leave his home, but thankfully he did not.

A few hours after meeting Chris and Carolina, I get a phone call from Chris asking me a few questions, in regards to the sale of his property. I offered to place his property on my company site as an open listing. He graciously had me do so, and recommended I reduce the price to market his property by $50,000. I listed it for $649,000. In the back of my mind, I did not feel that it was competitive enough but I was glad that he listened to my advice to lower his price. Needless to say I did not receive a single call on the property. Fast-forward three weeks later, Chris calls me to ask me if I would be interested in listing his property exclusively and of course I was interested. He was getting frus-trated with all of the agents that were calling him to pitch him for his listing, and the lack of phone calls her was getting from direct buyers. I immediately came up with a comprehensive marketing plan to get the home sold quickly.

One of the hardest things to do when listing a property is to ask the seller to lower his or her price and expectations before it even hits the market. I am a firm believer that any property will sell if it's priced well; looks good and is marketed properly. After many back and forth conversations with the owners, they priced the property at $550,000. The first open house generated over 18 prospective buyers, but most importantly, offers! In general the starting offers were low. When entertaining multiple offers, prices quickly rose. The final contract price of the unit was $540,000, all cash.

In total the property was on the market for 21 days before it went into contract. The unit closed approximately 30 days after. Chris and Carolina did a great job renovating the unit. The property looked great in all of the marketing that we did. The key to the sale of this property was the effective pricing. Don't price your properties high and chase the market down with price reductions. Price it right first, and you will never have to do a price adjustment. In this market properties that are over-priced are not even looked at.

After the sale of their home, Chris and Carolina moved to the Miami area to start a new business venture. They "caught the bug" for renovating properties and selling them for profit. They started "flipping" homes shortly after. Because of their amazing personalities, hard work and creative spirit, it was no wonder that a major television network decided to produce a show on them, to showcase and all the trials and tribulations associated with "flipping" homes. The first season, at the time this book is being published, is scheduled to air.

After selling their first property in record time, I was hired to do it again. I am currently representing the sale of their last property in NYC. Their property is being listed for over $2 million dollars and is located in a fabulous neighborhood of the Upper West Side.

Sell your house fast with the right look

This past January my colleague Veena Trinh and I met with sellers Christina and Anthony. They owned a great one-bedroom one-bath coop located in the Upper East Side of Manhattan. Their property was listed on the market with another real estate firm for over six months and when the listing expired with little to no success, they ended up trying to sell their property on their own. They were unsuccessful in selling their property. They were a bit apprehensive to give the listing to another broker, because they were afraid of experiencing a repeat performance of the last brokerage firm. Upon our meeting with the sellers for the first time, Veena and I really took our time to see where the agents in the past had some success and where they had met failure.

Selling a property is not an exact science, but if the property is priced well; looks good, and is marketed properly, it will sell. With this in mind we explained our marketing and pricing strategy with them. Veena and I understood that if we were given the same property, with the same pricing, and presented the property to the market in the same way, we would probably get the same results and that was not our intention. After we explained what we would do differently to get the property sold, the owners signed the listing agreement with us the very same day.

The asking price of the property when it was listed with the previous broker was $560,000. I asked the owners to make a small adjustment in the price and we agreed that $545,000 would be the new asking price. Veena and I felt that this was a number that would generate a lot of interest and put the property on the radar of most buyers who are looking for a one-bedroom coop in that area. The property was 825 square feet, and we were asking $660 per square foot. We knew at that point that the property had a lot of value behind it because similar properties were priced in the $700 per square foot range and up.

The biggest change to the listing became the staging and the prepping of the property. Overall, the property looked good. It had a fully renovated kitchen with stainless steel appliances. The bathroom was renovated with up-to-date finishes and the spacious living room had great crown molding and beautiful wood floors through most of the apartment. These renovations took place in 2009, and some minor wear and tear on the property were beginning to show. The walls, the ceilings and the crown molding needed a bit of freshening up. Once we pointed out the renovation opportunities to the owners, they immediately hired a few professionals to get the renovations done. All in all, the total touch-up costs to them came to approximately $2000.

The next step to the property makeover was the staging. The property needed a new look and we achieved that with a simple cleaning, de-cluttering, and rearranging the existing furniture. We added a coffee table and brought in some accent pillows, a throw blanket, candles, and a vase with some flowers. This easy and simple improvement cost a whopping $100. Staging does not always take a lot of money, but it does take imagination. This improved the overall appearance of the apartment drastically.

The true test of the improvements to the property came during the open houses. The feedback from the potential buyers was that the property showed very well and they could clearly see the value of the property. On the 43rd day of having the property listed on the market, we had an accepted offer.

Before you list your home, make sure the home is in its best condition possible. Sometimes professional staging can make the difference of a property sitting on the market for six months to a year or selling in less than 30 days.

Getting a home ready to sell is not always the easiest thing to do. Many sellers have a hard time distinguishing the property that they are selling, and the home that that are living in. Sometimes, the owners have to break their emotional ties with their home and understand that their home is now just a property and a business transaction. I have seen it on many occasions that owners feel they have the best looking property in Manhattan, and that staging and de-cluttering is not necessary. One of my most favorite phrases I hear is, "A real buyer will look beyond all the clutter and the mess and appreciate the property for what it is." I cannot begin to tell you how wrong they are. If you were shopping for a used car, and there were two identical used cars sitting next to each other with the same mileage, but one was dirty and with a few scratches and dents and the other one looked well maintained and clean, I can assure you are going to choose the car that looks the most visually appealing. The same goes for real estate. A buyer will look at a property seriously if it is in move-in condition. Most buyers do not have the imagination to look beyond a mess. You only have one chance to make a first impression, so make sure it is a good one.

There is a popular phrase that exists among home-buyers nationwide that does not real exist in the Manhattan market, and that is "Curb Appeal". By definition "Curb Appeal" stands for the general attractiveness of a house or other piece of property as it is seen from the sidewalk. Agents trying to sell or evaluate a piece of property often use this term. In NYC it's very hard to use that term when describing an apartment. In the land of concrete, brick and glass you can never tell what is behind the walls of a building.

Since close to 90 percent of real estate searches start online, "NYC curb appeal" starts with pictures of the listing on the internet. A picture is worth a thousand words, so make sure the pictures speak well of your property. An agent who is serious about selling the property will do anything and everything to make that property sparkle like a diamond that it is.

Sell your house fast with the proper marketing strategy

Today, social media is one of the best modern selling tools an agent or a seller can utilize. If used properly it can increase the exposure of a property to a much wider market. In my opinion only a small handful of brokers currently harness the power of social media. Marketing a property for sale has gone beyond placing ads in the New York Times newspaper or a simple ad on craigslist. There are many other powerful sites out there that can capture the attention of wide audiences, such as YouTube, Facebook, Twitter and so much more.

For every listing that I represent I create video that showcases the property, the building and the neighborhood, and post it to my YouTube channel. As an agent, I believe that it is important to not just sell a property but to sell the lifestyle that the building and the neighborhood has to offer. After every open house that I host, I contact each and every individual agent and buyer and forward the video over to them so that they could get a second look. Over a weekend, the buyers could see dozens of properties, at the end of the day all of the properties seem to look alike. Now when you send your video to them they can immediately recall they experience they had at your open house. They could forward the video to their spouse that could not make it to the open house, or to their parents in another country who is may be assisting them in paying for the apartment. Typically when you leave an open house you get a piece of paper with a few pictures on it. When you leave my open house you get a show sheet and a video waiting for you when you get home.

When I go on a listing presentation, I make it a point to show the prospective seller what I can do to create the buzz that is needed to gain the mass exposure for their property. The video is always a selling feature that they really want. If you can provide the sellers with creative and unique marketing strategies, you will get the listing. If you could provide the buyers with a better buying experience, you will get the sale.

Last July, I represented a listing in the Murray Hill area of Manhattan. At an open house I was hosting for the property, I met a buyer who came with her broker. The buyer came without her husband. He was a doctor with a busy schedule and could not make it to the open house. The video I made for the property was sent to the broker, who proceeded to send it to her client. The doctor ended up loving the property through the video. He made it a point to see the property as soon as he could in person. The following day they made an all-cash offer on the property. The property was on the market for four weeks and closed approximately 30 days later.

ABOUT THE AUTHOR – *Paul Macapagal*

Working in sales since age 16, Paul Macapagal always knew he wanted to get into an industry he would find most fulfilling. Since 2006, that has been real estate. In 2005, when he was preparing to buy his first investment property, Paul realized he wanted to understand the New York City real estate market better, so became an agent and he loves the job. Now his mission is to help others understand the market, and make sound decisions based on their needs and finances.

Paul is a natural at helping people. He's also a great negotiator who sees both sides of the picture. Whether you are buying, selling or renting property, you're in excellent hands. "I never lose sight of my clients' goals," says Paul, who sets his standards high. "My clients expect me to be constantly improving my knowledge and service, so I am constantly retooling myself. I'm here to educate and navigate them through the market so they make confident decisions that ensure satisfaction and great value."

Paul sells and rents luxury condos, coops, townhouses and new developments throughout Manhattan. He is also a listing specialist for owners and landlords, and an expert in corporate relocation. Paul has accumulated personal experience as an investor as well, specifically in the furnished rental arena. He's sold residential and commercial properties, with clients ranging from Fortune 500 executives and Hollywood actors to UN Diplomats and Ambassadors of Foreign Countries.

When representing a property, Paul draws on his broad expertise to accurately price and aggressively market each client's unique home. He also takes full advantage of internet marketing and social media to generate wide exposure. Paul's command of technology is complemented by his talent for photography which showcases listings in the very best possible light. "I don't just show an apartment. I present it with care and meticulous detail."

Customer service has always been the backbone of Paul's success. He previously owned several businesses, worked as a professional photographer, and in various sales capacities. This set the stage for his outstanding record in real estate. Paul sold 16 properties and rented 11 in his first year, and was ranked in the Top 10 percent in the U.S. at his former company.

Contact Paul at www.PaulMacapagal.com.

SECTION II

PREPARING THE HOUSE FOR SALE...

CHAPTER 6

Make Way for a New Chapter in Your Life

By Janet Todrank Koressel

So you want to list your home for sale and get the best return on your investment? Doing a few things to help the flow of your home can increase your market value! I will share a couple of examples of techniques I have run across over the years.

I received a call to list a home that was expired. Another agent had listed it for sale, and it had not sold. The home was in a good zip code with a pool and a view. The sellers could not figure out why it wasn't selling.

When I walked into the house on Peppercorn Drive in Henderson, NV, the first thing I noticed was the furniture placement. The kitchen opened into a family room with a fireplace. The sellers however, had set up a formal dining table in the room. The formal living/dining room was being used as the TV area. The first thing I suggested was to use the rooms in the manner they were designed to be used.

We moved the dining table back to the formal dining area. We put a sofa and coffee table in the den area and made the fireplace the focal point. It was exciting to see the difference! We sold the home within 4 weeks of putting it on market. It doesn't matter how beautiful your furniture is, if the rooms do not flow, the buyers are going to walk in and walk right back out!

On another occasion, I was asked to list a home for sale on New River Drive in Henderson, NV that had expired with another agent at a listing price of $499,000. The sellers had bought another home and were now carrying two mortgages. They were desperate to sell the empty house! It had been sitting on the market for six months, and it was in a beautiful gated community.

The home owners and I freshened up the areas, and used some decorator items. We placed brown towels with raffia in the restrooms, fresh flowers on the porch, a sign that read "family" on a ledge, installed a mirror above the beautiful fireplace, and opened up all the blinds. We also removed all of the solar screens, because the natural light was being blocked from coming into the home. (We are in the desert of Nevada, so we use solar screens to keep the homes cool in the summer – but the screens need to be removed when the home is being shown for sale.) After doing these minor changes, we put the house up on the market for an even $500,000. The home sold within 12 weeks for $475,000. Buyers want light! The house "flowed" better with the open windows and light shining through!

I had a listing in North Las Vegas, NV that was a great 3-bedroom starter home or investment property. When I walked, in I was taken aback by the red walls the sellers had painted. When I suggested that the sellers paint the walls a neutral color, they were not excited about the opportunity to put more money or work into the home they were leaving. We listed the house and had a lot of people walk through – a lot of traffic. We did not receive a single offer!

After so many potential buyers walked through the house without offering any nibbles, it was time to do something. The sellers decided they would paint over the red walls. They chose a great desert tan color. We took the house temporarily off the market. We started over, once everything was finished. This house looked like a different house! It felt much bigger and more open. An investor scooped it up right away, and rented it out immediately. Basically, buyers prefer not to have a lot of work to do when they buy a house. If you're selling the house "as is" the offers will reflect the condition of the home. Even small investments, like paint, will put money in your pocket at closing!

You've heard, "You only get one chance to make a first impression" over and over again. Remember that phrase when preparing your home for sale. Do you have curb appeal? Is the front yard free of weeds? Is the front door clean and inviting? Small touches like fresh, bright, flowers on the doorstep will be instantly "eye friendly!"

When you are setting the mood to show the inside of your home, turn on the lights, open the windows, and make it smell good! Vanilla is the best scent to use because most people like it. Make sure to keep the center of your rooms open and free of clutter. Arrange the furniture so the middle of the room is not blocked in any way. Buyers love open, flowing, uncluttered living areas.

Look at all the areas with a fresh eye, and ask yourself if the spaces are inviting and welcoming.
Declutter, de-personalize and pack up any of the memories you're taking with you. When in doubt, less is always more! All you need is one good offer! Your energy is the best marketing tool out there for your home! Buyers will feel the love you've put into the house to make it a home and you will see the difference in how fast your home sells and for the best price!

ABOUT THE AUTHOR – *Janet Todrank Koressel*

A thirst for a challenge, a desire for growth, an investment in lifelong learning and a commitment to customer service are what drive Janet Todrank Koressel.

Janet was born and raised in Indiana and attended Western Kentucky University and Southern Indiana University. Her passion to serve others and wanting to expand her knowledge led her to the airline industry. She traveled for 20 years and maintained successful relationships with a variety of people. She traveled to six of the seven continents while working in first class around the world.

Janet retired from the airline industry, got married and had a son. She works for Realty One Group in Henderson and Las Vegas, Nevada. She has over ten years of experience in real estate. She is a member of the National Association of Realtors®, and the Greater Las Vegas Association of Realtors®. Janet is short-sale certified and works with both buyers and sellers.

Janet's message to her clients: "I have embraced life's journeys and welcome the opportunity to serve you with your real estate transactions. The privilege of working for you is always mine, because Dorothy had it right: 'There's no place like home!'"

Janet can be reached at 702-612-3661 or at www.JanetKoressel.com.

CHAPTER 7

Preparing the House: Freeway Noise and Waterfalls

By Vera Brodsky

Location! Location! Prepare the House!

Since childhood we have been taught that home ownership is the "American Dream" and "Location, Location, Location" is the next best thing! But is that really true? Are people willing to pay premium for a house that is not a dream house, but the location is where their heart is? The answer? It is complicated!

A Young Buyer

A young single guy decides to buy his first house. His parents are there to help him and guide him through the process. With his parents' advice, he concentrates on location and not the house. He finds a house in one of the best neighborhoods of Seattle, with great schools, parks, easy access to freeways and all around location, location, location. But in the excitement of his first home purchase, no one notices the road noise from an arterial road bordering the house. The home has freeway noise too, and has an odd design with a few bedrooms downstairs, a few bedrooms upstairs, and a third level that makes for many, many stairs.

The years go by and he meets the love of his life! They decide to get married and she needs to move in but she hates the house. Everyone knows that good marriage lies in a happy wife, so they need to sell! And sell fast.

On a Sunday morning I get a call from her saying, "We are ready to sell. Come help us." Without hesitation I jump in the car with my real estate kit (my brain!) and off I went to see the home to be sold.

Once we had toured the house and pointed out the positive features (Location!) the work started on making the house appealing to the buyer.

- **Price!** Yes, price is the main selling point. You don't want to price it low, but pricing a house high will make you sell it low. The longer a house sits on the market, the lower the offers you will receive. If you price the house right, you have high chance of getting multiple offers and actually selling it for more than you think possible. If you price the house high to start with, savvy buyers will wait for you to drop the price and then low-ball an offer right when you become exhausted, anxious, and ready to sell.

• **Smell!** Most sellers take time to make the house look nice, clean and ready to sell. But does it smell good? When you go into high-end department stores or hotels, you are greeted with this smell that makes you want to stay, shop and spend. And you know the smell before you even go in your favorite stores. Houses are the same. If you are a smoker or you have special cooking spices, your house will tell. Smell is the first sense people remember and feel before they even enter the house. I have seen buyers walk away from a house without entering because of the smell. You open the door, the smell greets you first. Don't let the smell ruin your home sale. There are many easy ways to get rid of smells, and they are certainly worth the time and effort.

• **Noise!** What did the builder think when they built a house next to the road? But wait, there may have been no road when the house was built. It does not matter who is to blame, you are the one who has to live with the noise and sell the house. What do you do? A few things can be done. They may not be cheap, but they might help you get the big bucks for the house you crave so much to sell.

  ○ **Windows** – expensive! Yes! But if a buyer walks into the house and has to speak loudly in order to be heard, you have a problem. Good windows will not only help with utility bills but give peace of mind to the buyer that once inside, they can enjoy the peace and quiet they have longed for all day at work

◦ **Water fountain** – Windows can fix inside, but what can you do outside? Water features are a great solution. Although water features will not completely get rid of the noise, they will help create a more constant sound. The buyer will concentrate on the calm sound of flowing water instead of cars going by.

◦ **Music** – once you have the house on the market, leave classical music on at the house. Not only will it make street noise disappear, buyers may think you have a high society upbringing and make the house even more appealing. They will think about house Karma and what kind of owners this house has experienced.

• **Furniture Layout** – does your house fit all cultures? That is the question you want to ask. As our society gets more diverse, so do the buyers. There has been much talk in the last few years of feng shui. I am sure you like your house as it is and never paid much attention to it. Well, now is the time! There are many aspects of feng shui and if you incorporate the staging and home preparation with this method of Chinese geomancy, you might get a monetary reward in the form of higher sale price. Buyers pay attention. Placing a plant or a mirror correctly can help the buyer feel confident about "good luck" of the house.

• **Paint!** Now your house smells like a good summer day, you have a water fountain in front of your house, and your location is great. Buyers are excited to go inside. They walk in....yikes!!! Look at the colors! If your house is move-in ready but colors are very personal or too strong – you need to change the colors. Paint is an investment worth making. Buyers are busy with work, kids, life. If they are looking for a move-in house, they want a move-in house without conditions! Make the colors light and welcoming but not white! White is the 1970s. A beige palette is always a welcome sight.

• **Let's just update the bathroom...** I have had sellers whose house entire needs updating but instead of putting it on the market "as is" or remodeling throughout, they decide to update just one bathroom in the house or just one room. Don't do this. If your house is in need of remodeling, clean it, price it well and sell as "old charmer" or choose to remodel the entire house. Not only will remodeling one bathroom not help you, it might actually hurt your chances of selling. When a buyer wants to buy a house and make it to their taste, they will remodel everything. If they see one bathroom that has been done, now there is a need to match the house design to that bathroom, and who wants to do that? The buyer may also think that your house price has a premium due to this remodel that they may or may not like. Do it all or don't do it at all.

• **Is it warm inside? Can I take a shower?** Inspection – that is the dreaded word of every seller. What if the buyer finds something wrong? Do I have to fix it? Do I have to give them money? What if the buyer walks, do I have to tell the next buyer about the results of the inspection? Yes, we all have the anguish of waiting to hear from the buyer's agent. But how can you as the seller take steps to assure the buyer that you have loved this house! Service it. You maintain your car. You give it annual check-ups (or if you don't, you should) and your house needs a tune-up once in a while. What should you do? Well, here are few items I would suggest as most buyers know that the house will have minor imperfections, but it's the bones that they are worried about.

- Service your furnace
- Change your filter
- Service your water heater (replace it every 7 years or so)
- Check the attic for any roof leaks (if found, make sure you fix the problem and provide buyers with verification and assurance)
- Check the crawl space for any standing water (this is a big issue in the Pacific NW. If you do find standing water, make sure to have the problem solved by a professional company with a lifetime guarantee. Inspectors will see the water spots and you will need to show proof that it all has been corrected)
- Check your kitchen appliances to make sure they all work

- Check under the sinks throughout the house to make sure there are no leaks
- Caulk around showers and tubs
- Caulk, if needed, around the sink kitchen
- Check for faucets to be working

Do you still want to know what happened to my sellers? The young couple? Yes, you guessed it, the home sold! Why? The home was presented as though it was loved. We had great pictures taken by a professional photographer, and it smelled good! Yes, it did!

Are you ready to sell your house? Here is another tip for you – get the house just right. If you want to live in your house, someone else will as well. I have many sellers whose houses we re-arranged prior to selling, and sellers would tell me: "Gosh, now I don't want to sell, I want to live here" That is a home that will sell the fastest!

ABOUT THE AUTHOR – *Vera Brodsky*

Vera Brodsky's real estate endeavor started in 2006 when she decided that she needed a more exciting career than being a government employee. With a degree in Economics in hand and bilingual skills (she is a native Russian speaker), she plunged into the unknown sea of real estate, that was already starting to dry up. Although many agents felt that job was no longer feasible due to the bursting real estate bubble, she saw a challenge that she could not pass up! If she could succeed in this economy, she knew she would thrive once the market rebounded! The down market taught her a lot of things: most importantly to work hard, know the clients, know the business, and be patient. In this ever-changing career, she always feels challenged and that's what keeps her on the right track.

You can reach her at vera@verabrodsky.com.

CHAPTER 8

Focus on the End Result

By Terri Vellios

When it comes to selling your home fast and for the right price, what *not to do* is as important as what *to do*.

Keep in mind what attracted you to your house when you purchased it. I've found in many situations the person who is attracted to a house has similar taste. With that being said, you want to cast the largest net possible so as to capture the interest of the best buyer most likely to purchase your house. So from this point on don't consider it your *home*. To you it is now a *house*, and to the future buyer it will be a *home*. This is the beginning of the letting go stage. You can't sell something as long as you are still attached to it. So, start packing as if your house is sold and you are moving on.

The next step is to get all your inspections up front. This will give you control over repairs. You can repair what is needed and have an understanding of the cost to repair items that you are not willing to repair. This you can factor into your marketing price.

Sometimes it's the little things that make the biggest difference. Prepare the front curb appeal, front door, exterior, and inside by cleaning, organizing and depersonalizing. One of the best improvements, not costing a lot, is to remove wallpaper, apply fresh paint, and expose wood floors.

The Case of the Squeaky Floor

A few years ago I was helping a young family find their first home. They were looking in a specific neighborhood and the number of homes available (inventory) was low. We found a newer home for sale, and in the same complex, there was a home for–sale-by-owner. I contacted the owner to get a tour of the home. It was an interior location. The finish work was standard builder grade and the bedroom windows looked out over a shopping center with fast food restaurants.

The other home that was listed on the Multiple Listing Service faced a more traveled street, and the bedrooms faced the more desirable interior of the complex. This seller had paid extra for beautiful upgrades, which included cherry wood floors throughout. The home was also professionally staged to showcase the upgraded features and highlight the best use of the floor plan. The buyers decided to purchase the upgraded townhouse.

A couple of months later I was contacted by the owner who was trying to sell the home but had not succeeded. His house had been on the market for over eight months with two different brokerages after he tried "for-sale-by-owner." The last brokerage was a *help-a-seller* type of brokerage. After the listing expired with no results, the owner contacted me to market his townhouse.

By this time, the owner of the home had purchased another home and had moved out. He and his wife were carrying two mortgages. When consulting with the couple, I discovered that they were planning on starting a family and they needed the money from the sale of this townhouse. They were ready for a quick sale.

Because I had recently worked with a buyer for this type of property, I was very familiar with the similar homes that had been on the market and the homes that were currently on the market. It was important for the seller to be strategically priced to be competitive with the houses that had recently closed, those pending, and the current homes for sale (the direct competition). Even though this house was not located on a busy street, their location was not as desirable due to it backing up to a shopping center. Also, because it only had the standard builder finish, the value was less than the home sold to my other client.

The seller decided to focus on price and they elected not to stage. My efforts were on creating the house brand to attract buyers and buyer agents. A personalized website was created specifically for the townhouse. Professional photos highlighted not only the interior, but also the beautiful common areas, including the pool, and the lovely flowers and landscaping. Links inside the website introduced potential buyers to the local schools, the scores for those schools, neighborhood events, and the local amenities. Details of the interior finish work were featured room by room. In addition to the property features, the seller paid for the home inspection and pest inspection up front. These two reports, along with the required seller disclosures, were uploaded to the website so that potential buyers would have a clear understanding of the property condition. In the event any work was called for in the reports, the seller was prepared to make the corrections. Fortunately, being newer construction, the reports were very clean and few repairs were needed.

Then, I had individual business cards created that listed the property website. These business cards were handed out while touring other homes. The cards were also given out to buyer agents at networking events, and the seller was provided a stack to share as well. I also knocked on neighborhood doors and hand delivered open house invitations. This complex did not allow visible for-sale signs on the street.

Two types of fliers were designed for the home sale, an online flyer and a traditional flyer. The online flyer was emailed to all the local real estate agents. This flyer was also used to market the website on the internet, including Realtor.com, Trulia, Zillow, Craigslist, Google, Yahoo and numerous other real estate focused websites. The paper flyer was used at the home.

All marketing material directed buyers to the personalized property website. The property website has a lead generating capture window. Buyers had the opportunity to request a showing, or further information, and when a potential buyer completed a text, an email was sent to me so that I could give a quick response. Also, a "home-feed-back" form was put into action that allowed me to email each interested person quickly as to any changes with the property, and to send email invitations regarding upcoming open houses or expected offer date.

The first open house had a lot of activity and the comments from visitors focused on a squeak in the upstairs landing. We received an offer right away! Unfortunately, it fell out of contract. Because it was newer construction, potential buyers thought the squeak was a defect.

I had my handyman pull up the carpet to find a simple affordable fix. He installed a few screws into the floorboards, and he stretched the carpet back into place. The seller then made a price adjustment to reposition the property in the market. The seller also offered to provide a one-year home warranty policy for the buyer. The home warranty would cover several items, and give the buyer peace of mind. The following weekend I scheduled another open house. Utilizing the database of interested buyers and buyer agents, I contacted those who visited previously, and again marketed on the internet. This resulted in a lot of visitors and the seller received an additional two offers to choose from – all within 28 days of being listed. The home sold! It closed escrow 30 days later.

Funky Funky Floor Plan

One of my neighbors approached me to help her sell a rental house she recently inherited through a trust. The tenants had moved out. This eliminated one of the biggest obstacles in selling a rental house. During our consultation, my client revealed that her goal was to sell it fast, as-is, and minimize liability. She understood the required disclosures, and she was concerned she wouldn't be able to adequately disclose the condition, as she never lived in the house. I explained that by ordering pre-inspections to give to a buyer, she would be able to share information about the condition of the home. Those inspections also would allow her to make any required repairs prior to entering into a contract. Also, since she preferred an "as-is" purchase, the inspections would give potential buyers an understanding of the condition of the home, so that when they made their offer it would be based on knowledge and acceptance of the known conditions as opposed to any surprises and potential renegotiation during escrow. The inspections were ordered.

Then I connected her with the title company right

away. Since the property was in a trust, it was important that we insure she had the right paperwork and the proper authority to sell the house prior to receiving an offer. The escrow company's title officer requested a copy of the trust.

The seller made some of the repairs and removed the dated carpets to expose the original wood floors. She did the labor herself, saving money.

During my initial walk-through of the home I mentioned the biggest challenge was the "funky" floor plan. It was a split-level house. There were five steps to get to the front door. Once inside the house, there were two sets of steps, one set of about six steps down and the other set of seven to go up. The main upper level had two bedrooms plus a bath, a large living/formal dining room (which was listed as a bedroom on the county records) and a dated kitchen tucked away in a corner. The dining room had a deck that looked over the backyard swimming pool. The downstairs had two bedrooms, a bath, an inside laundry room and a very large family room including a wood-burning fireplace.

The house was located in a good neighborhood with good schools. For the list price approach, I explained that we needed to focus on the nearby homes which had the same floor plan, while eliminating the statistics from the other more desirable floor plans from the equation. There were three similar properties that had sold. With the revealed wood floors, minor repairs, and fresh paint and carpet, the home was ready to market.

When I prepare a home to sell I sit in the home and imagine who will buy this home. What do they do? How do they live? Because the house didn't have a formal dining room, the fifth bedroom on the main level was perfect to showcase as a formal dining room. This bedroom had a deck and double entry doors. The downstairs family room opened to the pool, and the laundry room was sizable. I decided that instead of calling the floor plan funky, I would call it versatile.

The split-level home could easily accommodate two families. I wrote up note cards with the following phrases "Imagine this room as a master bath." "Imagine the laundry room in the garage". "Imagine this room as a kitchenette." "Imagine a door separating the floors for privacy." "Imagine this room as a bedroom." Each room was re-purposed with dual functionality. I used the possibility of the floor plan in my marketing. Many potential buyers don't have vision that sees beyond the present condition. For this house, I used my words for virtual staging.

With signs in place, the home was placed on the weekly broker tour and weekend open house. The following week we received two offers. The seller chose the highest and best offer. It was accepted "as-is," and escrow closed in 31 days, with only a total of 36 days from being placed on market. Success!

Litigation Issues

Selling a condominium when the association has a

pending litigation against the builder creates a big problem. Problems occur for the buyer obtaining financing. A lender does not want to loan on a property when there is a lawsuit, whether or not the lawsuit has merit. A seller will either need to find a cash buyer or find a hard-money lender, also known as a private party loan. A cash buyer in this situation isn't going to pay market value, as they do not know what the value of the property may be in the future when or if the litigation is complete. A savvy seller willing to be resourceful has an opportunity to consider carrying the note. This will give them a down payment, and relieve them of their monthly costs such as home-owner's fees, property taxes, insurance and utilities.

Off the Beaten Path

A lovely family needed to sell their beautiful newer Victorian style home, located in the foothills in the Silicon Valley area of California. This is one of about a dozen homes I've had the opportunity to market that I would love to own myself.

As I put marketing into place that was along the lines of all of my marketing efforts, I kept thinking that there had to be something more I could do. I have past experience working with a developer, and what I like about what they do for new construction is to utilize renderings to showcase homes that are not yet built.

A light bulb went off! I decided that I would replace my street signs and open house signs with a photo of the home. A regular real estate "for sale" sign on busy street didn't have much of a call to action. So instead of my name and company logo, a large photo of the home was placed on the street with the property website. Then, when I had the open houses, directional signs also tied into the theme with a photo of the home so that those driving by would be drawn to the beauty of the exterior of the house and lead them to want to see the inside.

Then I decided that this wasn't quite enough, because if potential buyers were driving out in the foothills they would not know about this lovely home. So I paid to have the home featured on TV in town with advertisements that started during a busy St. Patrick's day weekend, and for the entire month following. The ad ran in local real estate magazines, and I also placed fliers in local shops. Then I put it on a special tour.

As luck of the Irish may have it, a local resident ended up purchasing the home. Looking back, I cannot say for certain how they learned about the house for sale. I do know that the more someone is exposed to something the greater chance they will follow up on it. You may have seen the Christmas movie "Miracle on 34th Street" where a little girl dreams of having a home. She finds one in a magazine and asked Santa to bring it to her. While driving through a neighborhood she begs her family to stop because she sees the home she envisioned.

This can be done in reverse as well. When you decide to sell your home, you can set up a vision board with a picture of your home and a sold sign in front of it. Place all the reasons you have for wanting to sell surrounding your home. Then place your vision board in a place you will see it every day. In addition, have each family member contribute to the vision board. You can take this one step further and invite family members to wear a "reminder-sold" bracelet, as a constant reminder to focus on the end result. The likeliness of any success is that much greater when the focus is on the end result.

You too can sell your home fast and for the right price. First move out of your house – even if it is only mentally. Focus on the reason for the sale and the desired end result. Prepare your home to attract the most buyers. Think outside of the box. And finally price and market it it right for the location, condition and market.

ABOUT THE AUTHOR – *Terri Vellios*

"I am the youngest of three raised by a single mother. We moved almost every year until I was 12. At that time I realized that people not only lived in houses but owned them as well. I remember sitting on the balcony of our apartment patio and watching classmates walk home from school. I longed to live in a home, but it seemed so far out of reach for a single mom to provide. To me home represented family, stability, and memories."

When Terri Vellios and her husband decided to purchase their first home, they needed the help of family, as interest rates were quite high. The first offer they wrote wasn't accepted. The agent representing then really didn't guide them, prepare them, or explain what happened. They found another agent who worked hard at finding a house and worked with them through a smooth closing. "Sitting in our first home on moving day without furniture was surreal," Terri reports. "I couldn't believe that it was our home and we could do anything we wanted to it, even paint the walls." Years later when it came time to sell, she remembers crying as they signed the contract. She's never forgotten those experiences. She likens the purchase of a home to a marriage – it is filled with new beginnings and hope for the future. She compares the sale of a home to divorce – years of memories are left behind, and there is a sense of loss. They have bought and sold several homes since then. Every time she works with a client she grounds herself so that she may tap into her own personal experiences and prepare her clients for what to be expect.

Terri Vellios is a full-time Real Estate Broker licensed since 1998. Her background includes new home construction along with resale. She takes a hands-on approach and zeroes in on her clients' goals, and together they establish a plan of action.

Contact Terri:

TerriVellios@comcast.net

www.TerriVellios.com

(408) 482-1800

CHAPTER 9

Clean the House and List it Like a Bank

By Julie Baldino

If you want to sell quickly and for the most money, think like a bank!

Bank-owned or foreclosure properties account for about 70 percent of the homes I am selling with my current listing inventory. I have learned so much from examining the process of selling a bank-owned home.

In my experience, banks are looking to ultimately liquidate houses (described as assets) as quickly as possible for the highest price. With all of the trusted advisers, attorneys, accountants, and experts that a bank employs, it makes sense to mimic a few of their sales practices to maximize the profit on your own home sale.

Know the property, know the target buyer

I distinctly remember my first bank-owned listing opportunity. It was a re-assignment, meaning that another agent had the property listed for several months and did not sell it. The bank needed some fresh perspective and innovative marketing ideas for selling the property.

I looked up the address on the Multiple Listing Service (MLS) and discovered it was in a fantastic neighborhood, surrounded by half-million dollar, historic, river view homes. However, upon further investigation, I found that the property had no view and was about 50 percent smaller than the neighboring homes. For me, this presented an excellent opportunity. When a home is in a fabulous neighborhood, it can sell well because location is a key indicator of a home's ability to be sold easily.

The drive to the property was through tree-lined streets, well-kept mid-century homes occupied by original owners, colorful landscaping, and charming architectural details. I am still confused as to why, even at the relatively high price of $175,000 this home had not sold. When I pulled into the driveway, the puzzle started to come together. The grass was three feet tall. A fir tree hung over the roof. The siding was rotted. Rats were actually scurrying across the driveway. And, the garage door was busted open.

When I opened the door, I was hit with three impressions. I smelled dog (or rather, multiple dogs), I smelled smoke, and I could smell the debris littering the living area. The house needed major cleaning and cosmetic remodeling, as it was in its original 1952 condition. The back window is busted. People who did not own the home were sleeping in the house, cooking food over a fire in the kitchen sink, and there was a rather large rodent infestation.

After a thorough examination of the condition, I determined the home was not suitable to be purchased for an owner to occupy, unless the owner was ready to perform a huge number of repairs. The price needed to be lowered to attract an investor or contractor who was capable of handling the scope of work needed. The updated calculations for repairs turned out to be roughly $50,000 to $60,000. The home had good bones and could be transformed back to beauty with an overhaul. With this new information, it was re-listed at a very reasonable price of $125,000. With multiple offers, the home sold to a cash investor in one week for $127,000.

One of the most valuable services I perform for my clients is a weekly property inspection. In this day and age of rampant vacancies, much can happen to a home if left unattended. In this case, the bank seller was not clear about the actual condition of the property. The seller wasn't able to make an educated decision on pricing the home without an up-to-date and personalized look at the condition of the home.

Scrubbing Down to the Bones!

Many people have the impression that all foreclosures are filthy, smell bad, have broken windows, are missing appliances, and worse. This may be the case in some areas, or in the past, but institutions (large and small) are starting to look more closely at conditions. It's becoming increasingly important for bank owned properties to be "show ready," mainly if the target buyer for that property is an actual homeowner.

However, the term "investor" has been expanded in today's day and age. It no longer applies to the landlord that owns 30 rentals, or the contractor that flips houses for a living. More and more "average Joe" type buyers are entering the real estate market as investors, due to low prices and competitive interest rates. As a result of this change in the target buyer pool, more homes are being targeted as "investor" properties.

When I first started in the REO business, I listed a home in Southeast Portland with a half dozen illegal additions and multiple code violations for poor condition. In my professional opinion, the home was probably only worth the land it stood on. It had been cleaned, debris removed, winterized, and deodorized. Still, the roof was leaking water all down the walls, the flooring was removed, mold was growing throughout, it was missing windows, the porches were falling off, etc... the place was a complete wreck.

A contractor hired by the bank met me at the property to assess the cleaning job done by the previous cleaning crew. When walking through the house, he started pointed things out that were NOT acceptable.... a cobweb way up in the corner, a missing air freshener in the kitchen, a small pile of debris in the attic. His response to being so particular was that every home should be presented in the absolute best light, so the buyer can *see the potential.*

No matter how disastrous it may seem, every house deserves a scrub down from floor to ceiling, and should always smell good (even if that means removing carpet). Appliances, mirrors, windows, and cabinet fronts should be polished, all clutter and garbage removed, yard mowed and edged. Without all of those distractions, the true potential of the property is visible.

Cost to carry...

As an agent working with a bank, I find that they are timing everything. The bank seller allows 24 hours to change the locks and take the initial photographs, 48 hours to get three repair bids, and 72 hours to conduct a thorough evaluation. If I do not abide by their rapid timelines, I lose the account and get no more listings from that bank. When you own real property and your goal is to liquidate that property, time is money.

Sellers all have "holding costs" on properties. Not just the payment, but routine maintenance, insurance, heating and cooling, etc. This should be taken into consideration when pricing a property to sell. The more payments that must be made (your holding costs), the more the profit margin goes down. Does it make sense to hold out for two months to receive $5,000 more, when your payment is $2,500 a month? Sometimes, lowering the price is as simple as doing the math.

Lowering the price will reduce the days-on-market. Lowering the number of days the property is on the market decreases holding costs, increases your net profit, and allows you to move on more quickly. Not to mention the fact that once a house has been sitting on the market for a while, people start to wonder what's wrong with the house, and the chances of selling decline rapidly.

Making the right decision on an offer...

One of the most valuable negotiating strategies banks utilize is waiting to decide on a bid, or requiring an asset be on the market for three to five days before they will choose an offer. Some of this is done inadvertently, as there are so many channels the proposal terms need to go through before a decision can be made. This practice, coupled with a very aggressive list price, can be a gold mine for a seller. Banks aren't afraid to price their properties low and wait a couple days. Why? Because they will receive fair market value (or more) anyway! Think about it... when a home is held for a short time, competition levels rise, bids start coming in over asking price, and the auction mentality takes over the buyer's psyche. Some of the strongest offers received on my listings were on day three or four, from a buyer that knew they were competing with five or six other offers.

Being in the right mindset...

When dealing with an institution, the transaction is completely void of emotion, which is advantageous to a seller. If emotion takes over, your ability to effectively negotiate is undermined. The goal is to reach a common ground where buyer and seller agree to all terms – a win-win. Again, in the opinion of the bank, this "house" is an "asset" that needs to be liquidated quickly and for the highest price. They do not get mad when a lower offer comes in, fuss, and/or refuse to counteroffer. An offer means that the house has an able-bodied and willing buyer, who obviously wants to own the home. There is always a "meet-in-the-middle" point with every purchaser. If an agreement cannot be achieved, they just move on to the next buyer without fear or regret.

The importance of professional photographs – the good, the bad, and the ugly

With over 90 percent of our buyers starting their search online, the first impression photo is *everything.* I have read that the vast majority of buyers will move on within three seconds if not captured by the first photo. As a case in point, I recently listed a beautiful acreage property in Battle Ground, WA that was owned by an appraiser. It had been on the market with a limited service brokerage for over a year, and had only a half dozen showings. It was priced right, because the seller had been a real estate appraiser for 20 years, and included significant improvements, like a brand new 1100-square-foot guest house. The grounds were wooded and beautiful with extensive water features; the home was tidy with a gourmet kitchen – an all-around great find! The problem? The first picture on the MLS was a photograph taken between the main and guest house (and seemed to be an attempt at trying to capture both structures with a cell phone camera) and seven subsequent pictures that made it look like a dump. This house needed a serious marketing makeover!

I hired a professional photographer, who came in and took about 150 photographs with a special wide angle lens, as well as a unique elevated stand that captures overhead photos. This allows the ability to capture multiple structures, views behind homes, surrounding acreage, and more. The visual effect is stunning.

A virtual tour was put together with our new pictures, and the home was listed the next week on the MLS (and blasted out on the internet) *at the same price*. Showings increased to about a dozen per week, and the home sold in 23 days at an open house. Not a single person that I talked to knew that it had been on the market prior to my listing it. Everyone thought it was a brand new listing because its market presence was entirely different.

So what if you have a really yucky house? An ugly house deserves pictures too, and investors are a large part of that 90 percent internet buyer pool. They want to see what's wrong with the house so they can calculate repair costs. So show it all off – the good, the bad, and the ugly. If the pictures scare a few buyers away, so be it. They weren't the right buyers for the home anyway.

Social media and the internet play a role in advertising your home...

Let's face it, you want your home to be seen by the 90 percent of people who look for homes on the internet!

For real estate agents, this involves manual entry on many different websites, the expense of photography and video, and is almost a full time job in itself. However, it is an absolutely vital tool in getting properties sold. In 2007, I started heavily studying "Search Engine Optimization" and I can attest to its success. I've sold listings from open house invitation videos on YouTube, from my Facebook page, Craigslist ads, and blog posts. Search engine optimization means describing the house using terms that buyers are typing in to seek the house.

It has also been recently discovered that buyers are searching for specifics, so they can bypass advertisements to find the house of their dreams. Unique features such as guest houses, acreage suitable for horses, outbuildings, specific school districts, and swimming pools should be included in the house descriptions. Video and photographs should be tagged with the property features and location. There are myriad ways to increase your home's visibility to potential shoppers, and agents should be utilizing every last one of them to find *your buyer.*

I highly recommend testing the internet savvy of your real estate agent by plugging in the address of one of their listings (in parentheses) on any search engine. For example, "124 Bella Vista" or "14808 NE 35th"... are there four pages of results, or forty? A stellar agent, who advertises on multiple venues, will have page upon page of results. Better yet, they will be able to provide you, the seller, with detailed reports about where your internet hits are coming from, which photos consumers are lingering on, and even what part of the country your lookers are coming from.

Create some hype!

I recently read an article that stated the best days to list your house are Thursday and Friday. If listed on those two days, studies show that your house will sell faster and possibly for more money. Since buyers are planning their shopping for the weekend, it makes sense that they would add the newest, freshest listings to their tour – maybe even go look at those first. I decided to test the theory, and took it a step further. Why not also hold an open house the following weekend? Why not send out invitations to the open house, put it on Craigslist, Trulia, Zillow, and in the newspaper? Of the first five I tested this strategy out on, three of the five sold to visitors at the open house, the fourth sold before the weekend, and the last had multiple offers come in on Monday – all at or above list price. List your house on a Thursday or Friday!

In closing, choosing the right real estate agent to assist you is absolutely fundamental to your home selling success. A knowledgeable, experienced real estate agent will be able to distinguish your target buyer just by looking at your home and neighborhood. They will be informed on the cost of repairs, and be able to provide proof of fair market value. They will recognize that photography and marketing should be a task delegated to professionals if they are not experts in those areas. Lastly, an excellent agent can analyze situations with a level head, and keep everyone calm so decisions are made in the best interest of the seller.

ABOUT THE AUTHOR – *Julie Baldino*

 Julie Baldino is a seasoned veteran of the Pacific Northwest real estate industry, and has consistently been in the top 10 percent of sales associates since 2003. She is licensed in both Oregon and Washington, and her specialties include listing bank-owned homes, short sales, investment properties, and new agent training. Julie is a Certified Distressed Property Expert Designation, Certified Negotiation Expert, approved Freddie Mac Credit Smart Trainer, and co-chair of the social media committee for Women in Default Services.

When not working, Julie enjoys spending time with her family and pets, vacationing at the Oregon coast, hiking, reading, cooking, and blog writing. She is heavily involved in animal related charities, a monthly World Vision and HSUS donor, and is the sponsor/assistant coach of a local girl's softball team.

In order to accommodate a rapidly expanding business portfolio, Julie recently opened her own brokerage, Front Door Realty, receiving recent recognition from the federal government as a certified "Woman Owned Small Business." Front Door Realty has grown into a solid team of buyer's agents, listing agents, and administrative staff. Utilizing progressive tools and innovative marketing ideas like social media, blogging, and SEO, the company is quickly gaining momentum in the Southwest Washington real estate market.

Front Door Realty is committed to exceptional standards of service, is a locally owned/operated brokerage, and would love to hear from you should you need assistance in the Pacific Northwest! She can be reached via phone, email, fax, and on the web at www.FrontDoorNW.com .

Office: 360-989-3390
FAX: 360-989-3389
Toll Free: 855-268-4115
Cell: 360-910-3586
Julie@FrontDoorNW.com

CHAPTER 10

A Little Staging Will Produce a Successful Showing

By Mary Faria

Pride of Ownership

It was a gorgeous morning when I sat down to discuss listing my seller's home located in the picturesque East Foothills, an area near the prestigious San Jose Country Club nestled in the historic Alum Rock Park area hills. This pocket area is like a spectacular shining jewel set in a crown of natural splendor, and is one of San Jose, California's best kept secrets. The prices can be up to one-third less than comparable homes on the west side of the greater San Jose area. This area has almost zero traffic, is only ten minutes away from downtown San Jose and most major freeway arteries, and in many East Foothill homes, you get the added gift of panoramic views of Silicon Valley and serene vistas of the adjacent countryside. Even though I've sold real estate from Santa Cruz to Hollister, and Gilroy to San Mateo in the greater San Jose area, this is the area where I choose to live and in which I specialize.

This seller is a prominent high school principal and a retired teacher. The teacher doesn't realize she is a self-taught interior decorator. The home on a scale of one-to-ten is an 11. They remodeled it down to the studs in 1991, and the house is still not dated. They maintained the flavor of its original 1939 build date, blending the old with the new into a recipe of absolute pristine beauty. I have never seen in my 13 years selling real estate, a turnkey house that exuded so much pride of ownership.

The sellers were moving to Oregon to retire. But before they moved out completely, they left behind key pieces of furniture and décor to sell the house in a beautifully staged fashion, from the antique hutch filled with serving sets of antique china down to the custom cozy pillows on the corner window seat. They agreed to price their house intelligently, and I marketed its unmistakable imprint of timeless country charm with city convenience, under breathtaking views of the city lights.

This home sold within $3,000 of the listing price with zero repairs, even though it sold during a Silicon Valley downturn in 2011.

I passed by the house the other evening, on the way to an appointment to list a neighbor's home. The new owner was out in the front yard, lovingly planting spring annuals near the rose garden where the area deer stop by for dessert every night. It brought such a smile to my heart, because I knew the house was again bringing bliss to its new master.

Pretty It Up

In the winter of 2011, I met with a seller in mourning. He was such a nice young man, an only child needing to sell a house that he had inherited from his father. He had lost his mother almost four years back, and his father had subsequently let the house go into disrepair with highly visible deferred maintenance. The seller had the overwhelming job of emptying out the house he grew up in. I felt for him. How emotionally difficult it must be to overcome the flood of memories from his parents' lifetime of possessions, while still grieving his father's death.

The house was full of personal property, and was in original 1970s condition, including single-paned windows, an avocado green kitchen with dark brown Formica "what-were-they-thinking" cabinetry, severely worn-out linoleum, carpeting far past due for replacement, an enclosed patio with peeling window-glare film, and very basic bathrooms. On the surface, it had very little panache, but it was a desirable four bedroom floor plan and fortunately it was in a good school district of North San Jose.

If we had listed the house in the above mentioned condition, the seller would have never realized top dollar. I suggested that we "pretty it up". Homes are like people. They are all beautiful. Some houses are beautiful on the inside, others on the outside. Some are beautiful inside and out, but most look better with a little make-up or grooming.

The beauty of this house was mainly on the outside, but it was covered up by dilapidated exterior paint and overgrown bushes that were hiding the lovely traditional exterior elevation. As a listing agent, it is my job to provide marketing that accentuates the sometimes "hidden" beauty and percolate it to the surface. Marketing is paramount to obtaining maximum market value. It will bring you the maximum number of potential buyers through your door. However, no amount of marketing will sell an overpriced house. Correct pricing at the onset increases the odds of a quick and successful sale.

The seller agreed to price the house competitively, and was very open to suggestions for preparing the house for sale. Over the holiday season, the house was prepped within a very limited budget, to get it ready to put on the market as the new year began. In Northern California, we see spring fever begin as January ends.

Curb appeal is the most important task for prepping your home, and the least expensive task that will garner you the highest return for your dollar is exterior paint. You have to get the buyers through that front door!

The seller hired an estate-sales specialist to sell the dated furniture and personal property that was left over, after he removed his cherished mementos. The bushes were trimmed to view the hidden flower-pot shelves under the front windows, and the low, rock-trimmed hardscape walls that framed what could be perceived as a front patio awaiting its flagstone floor.

The exterior was painted in an updated dark taupe color accented with vanilla trim, then the seller added a third paint color of black, to highlight the doors and window shutters, and to paint the 1970s style hanging entry light, immediately converting it from old-fashioned to high fashion. The interior was painted in two contrasting neutral colors. The house was professionally cleaned. Then new linoleum and carpet was installed. I then staged all the interior surfaces, as I now do for all my vacant full service listings. This staging included new and classic vintage decor for the fireplace mantle, kitchen and bathroom counters, towel bars, and the plain bathtub, fitted with an attachable wire rack complete with relaxing eye mask, sea sponge, bath brush, wine stem, and bubble bath bottle to add a *joie de vivre* flair.

The exterior was then staged with a welcoming floral door wreath and front door mat, and voila! This house was transformed from an ugly duckling into a lovely swan. The seller received 12 offers, and sold it for $17,000 over list price with zero repairs. Minimal money was spent on this updating and maximum dollar was realized.

There is a reason brand new model homes are staged. Even though new homes feature brand new open floor plans with innovative interior elevations, the sellers prepare beautiful brochures and stage eloquently. These new models are appointed with stunning décor and fabulous furniture because these companies understand a fundamental real estate rule for listing a home for sale or for rent. The way you live in a house and the way you sell a house is completely different.

A furnished house can be easily emptied of its clutter, professionally cleaned, and its furniture and décor pieces rearranged or moved to the garage, to transmute it to floor show mode and make it more buyer friendly.

A vacant house with an unattractive or outdated interior has no such option unless the seller has the money to either get it updated, or professionally staged.

It is strongly recommended if this is your case, that you ask the real estate professionals you are interviewing, for samples of their fliers to view their marketing abilities, and if they offer staging services for the surfaces of your vacant house, entailing built in hutches, niches, shelves or bookcases, fireplace mantles, kitchen, bathroom, and wet-bar counters, towel bars, tub surrounds, and even outdoor patio areas. The photos used for marketing your vacant house in a staged fashion will give potential buyers a sense of what is possible, and since real estate is now typically shopped for online first, it may make the difference between your house getting put onto a buyer's must-see list or not even making the cut at all. In most cases, all that is needed is a little sprucing up to the front exterior for curb appeal, paint, professional cleaning, and the surfaces staged to "pretty it up".

Realtor® Check-Up Tip

Ask the real estate brokers you are interviewing for samples of their marketing and a clientele reference list, just like you would ask of any other service provider you hire to work in your home. A good real estate professional will also give you their marketing plan up front in writing, before you sign their contract. It is California mandated that their real estate license number be on their business card. You can check their current status with the state at http://www2.dre.ca.gov/PublicASP/pplinfo.asp .

Sell the Lifestyle

When your home is marketed "For Sale" or "For Rent", the lifestyle it purveys should be marketed along with the property's amenities. The Multiple Listing Service in Santa Clara County, CA recently instilled a Walk Score. This is a rating of how easy it is to walk from the property to restaurants, coffee shops, grocery stores, parks, schools, shopping, entertainment, and more. What took them so long?! It has been widely established that both baby boomers and the younger generation of adults want and need to live a healthier lifestyle with today's hectic schedules. The internet, coupled with the electronic age, has brought us freedom with shackles.

We have access to unprecedented freedom of information, but are also shackled into spending so much time online. We all yearn to get back to a simpler time, where exercising was automatically built in to our lifestyle, and front porches were how we effortlessly socialized with our neighbors. This is exactly why certain areas are so alluring to buyers. They want to live near a downtown or plaza with quaint shops and restaurants, or be close enough to the recreation possibilities of a beach or lake. The majority of my younger buyers, ages 25 to 35, now prefer to live downtown for its' walkable lifestyle. This was not the case 10 years ago, before our downtown was fully re-vitalized.

Property Management

A duplex was purchased in 2004 that had a rear studio unit that was under city measure rent control. There were five other almost identical studios for rent nearby, so an inquiry was made as to what those tenants were paying, and it was considerably below the top of the rent control scale. I then marketed the lifestyle of the beach area where the studio was located, after staging the surfaces of the studio, and was able to attain a 33 percent higher rent than the neighboring five landlords. Never underestimate the power of marketing.

Pretty much the same principles that apply to listing your property for sale, apply to listing your property for rent. You need to price the rent competitively, provide curb appeal, get it professionally cleaned, and stage the surfaces of your vacant property to make the photos more appealing, in order to attract the largest possible pool of prospective tenants to choose from. Being a professional property manager and real estate broker, I have encountered many a landlord over-whelmed by problematic tenants. But this does not have to be the case. I have performed property management duties for over thirty years, without issues or evictions. The key is to rent to the right tenant from the get-go. Many investors fail to screen their prospective tenants correctly by not even running a credit report, and only going with their feelings. This is a mistake. You need to evaluate your prospective tenants by conducting a personal interview to ascertain why they want to move into your property, but you also need to see them on paper. If they have a good credit history, even if they don't have a lot of time on their current job, they will probably always pay your rent on time.

Rental Houses Need Love Too

In the late spring of 2012, a landlord whom had been using a family member as his property manager, hired us to take over the property management duties. The house was a darling cottage style with an enclosed front porch flanked by two columns, but it was extremely dilapidated with highly visible deferred maintenance, and the tenants had left it in complete disarray with debris everywhere inside and out. I couldn't even walk into the basement laundry room due to the pile of garbage left there. It took almost eight weeks for us to coordinate the remodel from top to bottom, but the result was an amazing phoenix rising out of the ashes transformation that resulted in a 35 percent increase in the rental income, with the landlord re-couping his re-hab costs within the first year.

I chose a warm cottage yellow for the exterior paint, ordered new windows, leaving the center bay window fixed with its stained glass transom, designed new front landscaping with scented cottage style flowers that included blue hydrangeas, yellow calla lilies, gardenia, fox glove, and a pair of yellow old English climbing roses for the charming front arch that we painted white, painted the interior walls, wainscoting, and cabinetry white to make it look like crisp clean linen, (I always use Sherwin Williams "Extra White" color), picture frame crown molding was added to the living room dropped ceiling to accentuate the gray green paint we used for the ceiling and drop area, and almost all surfaces were replaced in an antique noveau style, using white subway tile and new vintage style clear glass towel rods, doorknobs, cabinet knobs, drawer pulls, and light fixture shades. I found an inexpensive antique medicine cabinet with a glass door, built-in towel rod, and wainscoting backing to complete the look. I then staged the built-in living room hutch with green depression glass to match the green dropped ceiling, and the rest of the surfaces throughout in antique décor. The house looked too cute for words, and we absolutely had no problem getting top market rent for this cottage-style show piece. A little love and a little staging produced a very successful show! My favorite saying is "Love is all you need". We often think we only need to take the time to prep houses for sale, but sometimes rental houses need love too.

ABOUT THE AUTHOR – *Mary Faria*

Mary Faria, a Broker, says, "Real Estate and decorating have been a passion of mine from a very early age. I purchased my first home at age nineteen, with my husband of 34 years, and was hooked. My favorite game to play as a child was playing house, which grew into an innate love of feathering my nest. I enjoy filling my home with the things and people I love, and strongly believe our environment affects the way we feel. If we "feel good", we do good. I take pleasure in making potential buyers or tenants "feel good" when they enter my listings – so that the feeling they got when they viewed my online marketing or sign-post brochure is the same good feeling they sense when they physically walk into the property."

Mary Faria has been a Real Estate Broker Associate with Coldwell Banker for over thirteen years. She is trilingual English-Portuguese-Spanish, bringing 25 years of sales and property management experience prior to specializing as a listing broker, primarily in the San Jose and Santa Cruz, CA areas. She, along with her assistant/daughter Menina, a licensed agent with a marketing degree, do real estate sales and run a professional Property Management company, Faria Family Co. They owner manage a delightful Seabright Beach Vacation Rental in Santa Cruz California, the Sea Angel, decorated in Mary's signature vintage "beach chic" décor, which can be viewed at www.SantaCruzBeachRental.com. Her decorating style and 1930's Depression Glass collection were featured on the cover of the February 2010 issue of Today's Vintage magazine. The link to

the   article   is   http://www.todaysvintage.com/spotlight/
contentview.asp?c=265310 .

Her contact info and websites are:
Cell: (408) 206-7828
Fax: (408) 228-0571
Email: Mary@MaryFaria.com
Office: 2698 Berryessa Road, San Jose, CA 95132
www.MaryFaria.com
www.ColdwellBanker.com/for/Mary.Faria
www.SantaCruzBeachRental.com
www.Homeaway.com/398990
www.VRBO.com/186416

SECTION III

PRICING IT JUST RIGHT...

CHAPTER 11

Striking Just Right Pricing

By Mike Stott

When asked how to price a home so that it sells, I ask potential sellers this question: "What are you hoping to accomplish with this move?" Certain life events make a move mandatory (job transfer or family size increasing, for example) and some reasons to sell are wants rather than needs (downsizing or trading up, for example.) In either case, the goal in setting the price you will ask for the house is to get qualified buyers in to see your home and then to hear them say, "This house is the one – let's make an offer."

Pricing it just right means your home sells for the right price, in the right time, and with the right terms. Arriving at the right price can be a tricky piece of business. Price it too high and you'll get either no showings or showings without offers. Which means your price is helping some buyer decide to buy a different just-right-priced home. Price the home too low and you might end up giving away some of your equity (although there is a school of thought that says it may be impossible to price a home too low.) It's been proven that with proper exposure and marketing, buyers recognize a home that has been priced correctly. Buyers recognize a home that is priced too low, also. Sellers may even get into a multiple-offer bidding war situation and receive over full-price offers if the home is priced too low.

One example of just-right pricing occurred with a short sale (a property with a mortgage higher than the value of the home) that I listed for $274,000 in a neighborhood of $320,000+ homes. This 3,500-square-foot home was on a one-acre lot. It was a three-sided brick home with a ton of potential but it needed new appliances and flooring. In addition, the home had a swim and tennis clubhouse, and fed to some of the top schools in the state. The home didn't sell for three weeks. The owners decided to lower the price to $249,900. Within three days, we received three offers. The bank countered the offers at $269,000. With a short sale, the final price that is accepted is determined by the bank, not the sellers. One of the buyers accepted that price. Even though the home sold for $269,000 ultimately, $274,000 was not the right asking price. The home sale was priced just right at $249,900.

Just-right pricing is ultimately about the home generating an offer from a buyer who factors in a combination of current home supply and demand, their needs and wants, and market research when deciding to write up an offer. Home sellers will also typically need to be able to justify the price to an appraiser – since the vast majority of buyers need to borrow money to buy a home. The potential appraisal value should be factored into the just-right pricing equation.

I find that more buyers want to see a home that is priced right because it stands out from the competition on a quick price-versus-features overview. Right pricing effectively increases demand for the house. I find buyers are very motivated when they discover a new home on the market at a price that excites them.

I recently had a sale in which the sellers had already found their dream retirement home in Florida and had already purchased it. The sellers needed to sell their Atlanta home, a nice 4 bedroom, 2.5 bath ranch house in a great school district, in almost perfect condition. It had granite kitchen countertops, new appliances, fresh paint, and new carpet. The yard was manicured and simply stunning. They wanted to get to Florida! The sellers studied the home prices of the houses actively for sale on the market. They priced the home at the lowest in the neighborhood, but above some of the recent sales prices. I received three calls from potential buyers and one of them bought it with their agent right away!

Buyers today have access to more information regarding the real estate market than ever before. Buyers are conducting extensive research before making an offer. In order to price a home just right, I recommend you become the expert on home values for your market area. Define the parameters of your area. Is your area best defined by the school district, a city or town, or neighborhood? Ask yourself what a buyer from out-of-town would consider as the description of your home's neighborhood. Once the area has been determined, look at the competition. Drop by some open houses and get your real estate agent to tour you through the other homes on the market like your home, and get as much input as you can on pricing strategies.

Because of the sheer number and the effect they have on pricing, it is quite possible you may need to include short sales and foreclosures in your just right pricing analysis. When buyers came to see a short sale I was selling recently, they were surprised at the condition. They told me they thought "all short sales were gutted and run-down." This is sometimes true, but not always. In some cases a short sale or bank-owned foreclosure is in great condition.

When you look at all of the factors that will play into the pricing of the house, change your mindset from attached homeowner to detached "homebuyer." Look at each home you compare yours with through the "eyes of a buyer." Look at your competition with a non-emotional but critical eye.

Ask yourself the following questions: "In what ways does my house fall short? In what ways is it better? Why would a buyer choose my home over that one?"

Talk again to your agent about the sold prices of the

comparable homes nearby. You might want to ask your agent to factor in closing costs of selling a house that are paid by the seller. Use statistics if at all possible. Calculations like dollars per square foot, sales price to assessed price ratio, actual list price to sales price ratio, and list price being less than the last sales price are all useful in creating value in the eyes of potential buyers.

One tool sellers find useful is the Sell Your House Fast spreadsheet you can download from the www.Sell-YourHouseFastBook.com website. This gives you a good starting point for just right pricing and provides an invaluable way to show potential buyers and agents how you arrived at your asking price and why it's a good deal.

If your home is truly unique or there is not enough comparable to make an assessment, I suggest you hire an appraiser to give you, in writing, his or her professional assessment of value. This appraisal should be a tool that a buyer could take to a lender to obtain a loan. A certified appraisal will cost between $400 and $650 but is well worth it if you and your agent don't have enough info to determine the just right price.

I had a unique property for sale: 10+ level acres of land with a barn, a huge out-building and a 1940s style cottage with two huge additions tacked onto the back of the house. The condition was good but everything was out-dated. The owners were elderly and did not want to replace or update the fixtures, wallpaper, appliances and décor. There were no active homes for sale in the area and no sales of any home within 10 miles for over three years. The owners were seeking $450,000 for the house. The house appraised for $420,000. This was an excellent guide, so we listed it just below the appraisal value at $417,900 and it sold within 23 days.

Take some time to identify bragging rights for any home you are selling, so that it may stand out from the competition. Buyers buy emotionally. Buyers use bragging rights to justify their purchase decision, both to themselves, and to trusted family and friends. Besides the statistical bragging rights, other potential bragging rights include how much cheaper it is to own versus renting a similar home; finished basements at the same price as homes with unfinished basements; pools, media rooms, superior condition, and any other unique characteristics that you may be able to point out to the buyer.

Some buyers are unsure of making a large buying decision. If your home doesn't give the buyer the opportunity to brag to their family and friends what "a great deal they got because of '*insert your bragging right here*'" then you may not get a buyer at all. One way to figure out a bragging right is to remember back to what the seller liked about the home in the first place (when he or she bought the home initially).

The next step in pricing correctly is to make sure the price is appealing to other real estate agents. Since 90 percent or more of people buying a home will use a real estate agent to help purchase a home, it is important to make sure your home is perceived as priced just right to real estate professionals also. Look at the same sales comparables (information about homes that have sold nearby that are similar) and ask yourself how you can attract the agents to show the home. Advertising comments can go a long way towards showing the agent that this home is priced just right. Most agents search by neighborhoods, school districts or zip codes and then look at the list of homes sorted by price. If the home you are selling is not priced the lowest, make sure that the remarks highlight the bragging rights. For example, if you are selling a 5-bedroom home that is competing with a 4-bedroom home priced cheaper make sure you note that this house is the "LOWEST PRICED 5-BEDROOM IN NORTH ATLANTA."

In this focus on positioning your home to appeal to the buyer and the buyer's agent, I recommend that you steer clear from cutting the commission to the buyers' agent. The buyers' agent may have a lot of homes to choose from. If 10 homes for sale offer a three percent commission to the buyers' agent and the home you are selling provides a 2 percent or 2.5 percent commission, a buyer's agent may skip showing it completely. Make sure the home you are selling is priced just right, high-lights bragging rights, provides a competitive commission, and is the easiest house to show.

The last step is to remove all obstacles for a buyer to see the home. This will help the buyers make an offer. To make your home extremely easy to show, use a lockbox. Allow buyers to see the home the same day they would like to see the home. This means the house should be "show ready" every morning. Make sure all the lights are on, the blinds open, the trash empty, fresh flowers are out, and the home looks ready for a new owner.

There are many reasons for short-notice showings. Agents may have forgotten to set up showings the day before, or a buyer may have just driven by or noticed the home you are selling. When you allow short notice showings, you may find a buyer falls in love with your home without seeing the competition.

Here's a quick list of tools to have on hand when the home is being shown:

· Have a fact sheet ready for the buyer and their agent that show the buyer your estimated monthly utility bills based on the past 12 months.

· Get a lender or your agent to help with explaining the principal and interest payments.

· Provide a disclosure statement filled out and ready for the buyers review.

· Consider writing a short story telling why you loved the home and neighborhood so much and why you are moving.

· Present a list of all the extras in your home (say you spent $50,000 finishing a basement and adding a media room – itemize each expense and add it up so that they can see the cost and value.) These allow the buyers to brag to their family and friends about how smart they are for buying their new home.

· Explain the pricing by sharing the price of comparably sold homes.

In today's internet-driven world, a new home for sale is assessable to viewing online within 24 hours of being posted. According to the 2011 National Association of Realtors® (NAR) Profile of Home Buyers and Sellers, 25 percent of all homes are sold within the first 14 days of being marketed, and 37 percent of all homes will sell within the first 28 days. If the house does not get any acceptable offers for 21 to 30 days, ask your agent to take another shot at the statistics and do some additional research or conduct the research yourself.

If no homes are selling in your area or price range then there may not be a ready supply of buyers. Take a new look at your competition and make absolutely sure you are the best value on the market. If other homes similar to yours have been selling, then you are probably priced too high and should lower your price so that it is just right. If you receive no offers in 45 to 60, days then you definitely need to lower the price to find the just right buyer.

Following these steps is best accomplished with the help of a professional real estate agent. If you don't know of a great agent in your area, check out the excellent agents in the community at www.SellYour-HouseFastBook.com, and if we are not in your neighborhood, we can refer you to a fabulous agent in your neighborhood.

ABOUT THE AUTHOR – Mike Stott

Mike Stott, Realtor® CRS at Keller Williams Realty North Atlanta, has been selling real estate since 1980. Having helped over 3,000 people sell or buy their homes in Hawaii and Atlanta has taught him the importance of asking the right questions, really listening to the answers received, and then coming up with a solution to the challenge. He has won numbers of awards and is an author, consultant, coach (at YourCoachingMatters.com) and sales trainer. He can be reached at mike.stott@mac.com.

CHAPTER 12

When Sellers Win

By Niki Miller Maroko

My business partner, aka "Mom" and I park across the street from the house we are about to list. As we gather our belongings, my heart beats a little faster with excitement. My mother reminds me that Mikhail Baryshnikov said that he was always nervous before going on stage. For some reason, that always makes me feel better.

For this particular listing appointment, we have everything going for us. The sellers are a referral from a past client. Their home is located in the middle of the area in which we specialize, and the house is beautiful. We've been invited in. We've met their dogs and heard about their moving plans. As they take us on a tour of the house, I pay special attention to all of the pull-out drawers and cabinets. These sellers are clearly proud of the upgrades they have done. They are excited at the prospect of moving.

We sit down at the dining room table and go through our listing presentation, covering all of the major talking points. It all comes down to list price, market conditions and showing condition.

Our first step is to explain the importance of the listing price verses the selling price and how important it is to attract buyers to come to see the house. For some reason, this is difficult for many sellers to understand. For one thing, some sellers have a ballpark figure in mind when they sell their house. It's always important to discover what the seller's expectations are, so that we can try our best to meet them. Most sellers have watched the market for a while, and have attended open houses in the neighborhood. Many have compared their amenities to those of neighboring homes.

Phil and Denise watched their neighbor's house sell last year for $900,000 in Sunnyvale, CA, and it was the same floor plan as their house, but the home was not as nice. Recognizing the market has gone down a bit, they are hoping to sell their house for the same price. As we have done with every listing appointment, we have already pulled the title documents from our title company. We have conducted a comparative market analysis to determine fair market value. We have seen many of the homes that have sold recently, or are currently on the market. We have our recollection and the multiple listing photos to assist in our discussion on price and fair market value.

As we discuss list price, we explain to them that the price is set according to the market conditions. Right then, inventory was at an all-time low for Santa Clara

County. There were only 1,640 houses available on the market in the entire county – when a balanced market historically has been about 5,000 homes. In Sunnyvale that week, there were only 33 houses for a city with a population of about 134,000 people. Of those 33 homes, only about half fell within the Cupertino Union School District, a big draw to families in the area. As an example, we tell them about our listing in the Willow Glen area of San Jose. The area is nice and the schools are great. We had 13 offers and sold the house for $40,000 over asking. We know that Phil and Denise's house will sell fast, for a lot of money. It will do so in any market if we price it and show it appropriately, but especially in *this low inventory* market.

With that piece of information, they are more excited than ever to list their house for $900,000 and maybe even get *more!* But that is not the whole picture. We never try to tell a seller what to do, or ignore their feelings and thoughts. Instead, we provide them with statistical information, an analysis of market conditions, and thorough insight on the do's and don'ts of showing a property. In this instance, we were able to show Phil and Denise that there were two houses currently listed for sale in the neighborhood – one of which was a 3-bedroom, 1-bathroom foreclosure that had already been on the market for 90 days. It had sold and fallen through twice already. Phil and Denise's house has only two bedrooms, plus an office/den, but they have two full bathrooms and the house is 1506 square feet. The foreclosed home is listed for $799,000 and is 1700 SF. The only other available listing is a four-bedroom, two-bathroom, 2,200 square-foot house listed for $900,000. It has also been on the market for 30 days.

Phil and Denise agree that our list price would be simply too high if listed for $900,000 when there's a larger house with two more bedrooms sitting on the market for that price.

Let me clarify. If your house is really worth $700,000 (meaning, there was a house that sold recently that is very like yours in size and amenities), yet you price it for $650,000, you will get 10 people wanting it and it will be bid up to the $700,000 range. Many sellers are afraid that if they list the house too low, they won't have any chance of getting more for the house. I have seen sellers list their house $50,000 too high, then have it sit for 30 days, then they reduce it $20,000, then reduce it $20,000 again at 60 days, and finally sell it at 90 days, another $20,000 *lower than the originally recommended price.* If they had listed conservatively, they may have gotten two or three offers, or even just the one perfect offer at or within a few percent of the list price.

The point is, if you list your house even a little bit lower than the closest available comparable property, you are less likely to be stuck with just one buyer offering. If you do have one buyer, what is that telling you? It's telling you that is the fair market value of your house! The rule of thumb is that the highest and best offers come when the house has been on the market the first two to three weeks. If you don't like the offers you are seeing, waiting another 30 days is *not* going to help you demand more money for your house.

In Silicon Valley this year, we are lucky that we have a lot of buyers in our area and they will fight for the house. However, in any market, the downside of listing too high is that the house sits on the market and gets discounted due to length of time on the market. The downside of pricing too low is that you might receive multiple offers and over-bids. Of course, there are inexperienced agents who price their listings artificially low. That, to me, should be avoided.

How low is too low? Our rule of thumb is to price the house fairly, based on the median sales prices so that there won't be an appraisal problem. It's best to know what matrix appraisers are using to assess value. For example, when the market is slower, appraisers may look at the last six months of sales within one mile of the property. However, more recently, appraisers are generally going back only three months. Therefore, we determine value based on the median household sales price, within one mile of the property, within the last three months.

For the home that we are selling in Sunnyvale, we are also taking into account the larger foreclosed house five houses away and conservatively came up with a list price of $780,000. This is the price the sellers agreed to list the home for on our listing contract.

Now the fun begins! The condition of the house is very important. But even a house that needs work will sell if buyers know what they are buying, and if the house is priced fairly. We *always* encourage our sellers to get inspections up front so as not to "give away money."

First of all, we are always present for the inspections so we can learn about the product and be able to market it efficiently. We don't crawl under houses or climb up on the roof, but we do attend so we can learn about the house. For example, we will know if there is copper plumbing, where the furnace is, and approximately how much effective-life the roof has. If there are termites (which there usually are in California), we will know how much it will cost to eradicate them. This information is always good to know up front, before the house is on the market.

Once we know about the house, we are able to pass along the reports to interested buyers *before* they make an offer. This takes away the worry of something new being discovered. I had a client ask me last year, "But we had to do our own inspections when we bought the house, so why can't we just wait for a buyer to do their own inspections?" True, it's always a good idea to have a buyer perform, at the very least, a property inspection, so they may learn about the inner workings of the house. But they should not be the first one to discover if there is a major plumbing leak or the chimney is broken.

If you are a buyer, you may be okay buying a house knowing it will cost you $1,800 to have a fumigation tent. But if you make an offer and later discover that the termite work will cost you almost $2,000 more, you will probably not be too happy about taking on that additional cost. A broken chimney could cost you $5,000. That's a huge cost for a buyer. Again, if the buyer already knows that when they make their offer, they will factor that cost into their purchase price and may accept the house without expecting the seller to pay for these repairs – especially if there are multiple offers and they have to fight for the house.

Presenting a buyer with a complete package of inspections will make them feel comfortable putting forth their best offer *the first time* and will save the anguish of everyone discovering something wrong and having the price re-negotiated. If we don't do the inspections up front, the buyer may come back and re-negotiate the price. That's painful for the sellers, who have gotten mentally and emotionally invested in the sales price. This can also make repairs more costly and an inconvenience during the escrow period. For example, if you have a termite inspection before putting the house on the market and you discover a water leak under the bathroom toilet, you may decide to replace the very expensive tile floors with a lower grade tile, or vinyl flooring. If this is discovered by the buyer during escrow, you may have to repair and replace "like for like," which can be quite a bit more costly. When a seller conducts repairs and upgrades prior to putting the house on the market, he or she will have the choice of cost and materials.

At this point in our discussion, Phil and Denise asked us a very common question, "What if the inspections say we need a fumigation tent for termites? Do we have to do the work?" The answer is a solid, "No!" Once we obtain the inspections, we make a choice on what to do, based on deal-breakers and money makers. Having a leak in the roof could be a major deal-breaker for a client. Most buyers would rather buy a house that is leak-free and many roofers may even provide a 1-year leak-free warranty. Refinishing hardwood floors or applying fresh paint is a very good return of investment and can be a money maker.

We always measure and make recommendations about which work to do and not to do. We base the recommendations on doing work to take away a buyer objection (a deal-breaker) and doing upgrades to increase the value in the buyer's eye (a money maker). A seller may be bothered by the fact that the lights dim whenever he runs the dishwasher at the same time as the microwave, but it doesn't warrant spending thousands on electrical work. Disclosing this information to the buyer is enough to inform them of the nuisance and it may not be necessary to repair or correct the issue. The other reason to correct an issue is if it represents a health and safety issue. For example, exposed wiring in the attic that could be a fire hazard. This isn't a money-maker, but it could be a deal-breaker.

Another aspect of property condition is to make sure the house is clean and fresh. Most sellers are very aware that their house should be clean, vacuumed, dirty laundry and clutter picked up, and furnishings arranged in an attractive manner. There are books and magazine articles that cover the art of staging a home. If our clients need additional help on this, we have resources to hire stagers, furniture movers, professional organizers, clutter reducers and handymen. A good agent has an arsenal of talented, trustworthy and reasonably-priced referrals ready to hire.

For Phil and Denise, we had the property and termite inspections right after we went into a listing agreement. We had a contractor fix a small kitchen plumbing leak, install a ground fault circuit interrupter to the bathroom electrical outlet, and we put the house on the market. We had 102 people visit during Saturday's open house; 97 visited on Sunday. On the following Wednesday, we had 12 offers and the house was sold at a price of $825,000. They didn't quite get their price of $900,000, but their house was fully exposed to a market of buyers and they received the highest and best offer, in just seven days on the market. Victory!

ABOUT THE AUTHOR – *Niki Miller Maroko*

 Niki Miller Maroko is a 3rd generation Realtor® with a Broker license, a Master of Business Administration, and a BA in English from the University of California Davis. She is a Housing Commissioner with the City of Cupertino, an AYSO soccer coach and a director with the Silicon Valley Association of REALTORS®. She is a 2012 director with the California Association of REALTORS®. She enjoys playing soccer and softball, and loves to work in the garden. She and her husband Gil live in West San Jose, with their three children. Her mother, and mentor, Carolyn Miller, is a 30 year veteran of real estate.

Visit their web site at www.CarolynAndNiki.com.

CHAPTER 13

Home Sales on the Money

By Charita Cadenhead

A Lowball Offer Beats No Offer At All

Sellers make a grave mistake when they insist upon sticking to a list price that is not drawing any showings and therefore is not drawing any offers. I have advised sellers to lower their price because I know that a lower list price can still result in a higher sales price. At the very time of this writing, I am working on a transaction where the seller accepted the offer price and then the buyer increased that price in order to cover his closing cost. This has happened on more than one occasion. Actually, in real estate sales, it happens all of the time.

I remember my first year in real estate when a seller took my advice based on my conviction that lowering the list price ultimately had a positive result for the ulti-mate sell price. This particular home had previously been on the market for nearly a year. When it expired, I reached out to the seller. At the close of my presenta-tion, I walked out of the door with a listing agreement.

Based on the comparative data of homes sold nearby at the time of the listing, the seller agreed to price the home more than $7,000 less than the previous agent had listed the home. He was not quite comfortable with the new price, based on his assumption that the buyer would ask for an even lower price as well as the sun and the moon during negotiations. Within 60 days, we had a negotiated contract and the final sales price ended up being $5000 more than the original list price during this particular listing period. The buyer got the concessions that he wanted, and the seller got the net that he needed, and all were very pleased with the results.

In conversations with sellers about price reductions (particularly when there is staunch resistance), I find that the following points help communicate the reality that a price reduction does far more good than harm. I ask sellers to ponder these points:

- Do you want to keep the house listed at its current price and continue to get little to no showings?

- Do you want to lower the price and increase the chances of generating more showings?

- More showings equal more opportunities for the house to sell.

- Just because buyers may want sellers to come down on price does not mean that you have to lower your price. There is no hard and fast rule that says homes cannot and do not sell for asking price.

- Just because you will not come down on your

price at a buyer's request does not mean you will lose a buyer.

· An offer for less than a new price is far better than no offer at the current price.

Sold at the Speed of Light

I will never forget the time I listed an expired listing. There were two previous listings with a total of nine months on the market before I became the seller's agent. When the sellers agreed to list with me, they were surprised that my recommended list price was higher than their last list price. We are not talking about thousands of dollars higher, but higher just the same. I had the list of homes sold nearby (comparative sales data) that supported every penny of the suggested list price. Homes had been selling like hotcakes in that area. I could not understand why this house had not sold. After all, there were 21 traditional sales within one-half mile that had sold in the six months prior to my getting the listing.

The sellers said, "Let's do it." Staging was not necessary and the only thing the sellers really had to do was to make sure the home was show-ready at all times. After the listing went on the Multiple Listing Service, there was exactly one showing immediately, and within 11 days of listing the property, we had a contract. The icing on the cake was that in just 31 days after listing the home, the transaction closed. The sellers were over the moon, and to be honest, so was yours truly.

As a real estate professional, the absolute best that we can do for our clients and potential clients is to be realistic about pricing. As a seller, you gain nothing by overpricing a listing and refusing to come to grips with the realities of the market.

Price, Location and Condition Sell a House Faster Than Anything

In the end, when selling a home, price, location and condition will sell a house faster than anything. There is not much you can do about location if you are planning to sell your house. Perhaps it is in a prime location, but even if it's not in a prime location, if you really want to sell the house, then you need to price it right for the location and make sure it is in its utmost show ready mode at all times. Moreover, if it is an investment property, at the very least, you will want to make sure that it is not trashed.

Online Presence Is Equally as Important as a Personal Showing

If you do nothing else once the house is listed, have your agent email you a link to the Multiple Listing Service copy of the listing. You need to know how your agent is presenting your house to the world. Make sure your photos look good on the listing. Look at the listing the way a buyer would look at it.

Don't Be a Seller That Is Pretending to Sell a Home

There are many ways that a seller can disguise a listing as if it were really for sale, but in the end, the house is likely not to sell. The following are some of those ways:

- Grossly overpriced listings

- Lack of creativity in descriptions or no description at all

- Not enough information about the home itself in the description

- Lack of home features (where specific fields are available in the MLS)

- Unreasonable showing instructions (i.e., "available to show ONLY on Mondays and Wednesdays between 1 pm and 3 pm")

The best listings have:

- Photos that give a clear picture of the home's features and invite the buyer in the house

- Descriptions that go far beyond "won't last long" and talk about the bragging rights of the home

- Showing instructions with short notice where possible and not limited to specific windows of time

To put it all in perspective, selling a home is a serious matter and as a seller, you should approach it as such. From the start, you have to be willing to be an active participant in the process. Your input is always valuable, but no one knows the market and its condition like a real estate agent. After all, we live and breathe real estate and if other agents are like me, they even sleep real estate. As real estate professionals, it is our business to know the market. It is our business to study the market. It is our business to know the price ranges of homes similar to yours that have sold (we call them comps). It is our business to know what attracts buyers and what turns them off. We have firsthand knowledge of what buyers want and what's popular and what is selling at any given time. Every piece of advice that we offer you is based upon our knowledge and experience of our daily lives as real estate professionals.

ABOUT THE AUTHOR – Charita Cadenhead

Charita Cadenhead is a trusted and competent Realtor®. Bham WIiRE Realty is a small fish in a big pond. "I continually sharpen my skills and I am dedicated to my craft. Every client, without exception, gets the very best service that I have to offer. I am an independent broker and if ever I should seek to be an independent contractor by hanging my hat (license) elsewhere, you'll continue to get the very best in service. And THAT is my promise to you."

The WIiRE in Bham WIiRE Realty stands for Birmingham Women Investing in Real Estate. Chances are when you see that name or discover what the WIiRE acronym stands for, you don't get the entire picture. Empowering women through real estate is what we're about. That's the focus of Bham WIiRE Realty as it was originally intended.

One of the most fascinating aspects of working with sellers is the myriad of online opportunities that exist to market your property. With the proliferation of social media and blogging, as an agent, Charita gets to "talk up" your property frequently and extensively in a way that a single listing in the MLS does not allow. With online marketing your listing gets syndicated to hundreds of websites for maximum exposure. Charita's a firm believer in incorporating all of the latest advances in technology into her marketing mix and wouldn't dream of doing otherwise.

You can find find Charita on Facebook, Twitter and LinkedIn to name a few. Just look for chcadenhead on Facebook and bhamwiire on Twitter and LinkedIn. She has also been featured NuWireInvestor.com as well as Realtor.com.

In addition to the social media sites, her blog, www.bhamwiire.com plays a vital role in the marketing your property, but she also provides helpful information to attract buyers in general. The more information that she provides, the more she optimizes keywords, then the more opportunities that she has to draw buyers to your property.

Contact Charita Cadenhead at www.bhamwiire.com or bhamwiire@gmail.com.

CHAPTER 14

Open Up to Great Pricing

By Rebecca Selden

In the Bay Area of California, in order to sell a house, in the shortest amount of time, for the most amount of money you need to:

- Price the house correctly. The first time!

- Present the house well by eliminating clutter and sharpening the curb appeal.

- Market the property well. This makes it accessible to the buyer.

One of my favorite stories is about a working couple who were moving about 20 miles away. I sold their old home and facilitated the transaction on their new home purchase. I met this couple just by walking in my own neighborhood. This couple mentioned that they were thinking of moving. But first they needed to find a home they wanted to move into.

I made an effort to hand-deliver a few listings to the couple, and asked them what time Saturday they were available to go tour. But before we could tour I needed two things, to get their house on the market and make sure they were pre-qualified to buy a new home. They had the pre-approval letter for the new home the next day. I listed their house for sale, and we went to work on getting it ready to sell.

Thankfully, they were excited to sell and were open-minded about the staging of their house. Boy, did we have to de-clutter their home. They had accumulated a lot of things. When selling a home, it is important to have the house de-cluttered and de-personalized for several reasons. Not only does a clutter-free, non-personal, bright and light property show better, but it also allows potential buyers to imagine their own furniture and belongings in the space. It is essential to hide your medication and valuables when you are selling your house, also, for security.

Additionally, pre-moving allows access to areas that may have otherwise been covered and isolated. Creating space by de-cluttering works well for both the buyer and seller. The seller shows more clearly what they are selling, and the buyer understands the scope of what they are purchasing. Inspectors can only inspect what they can see; they do not do any heaving lifting or moving of items.

Anyway, back to the couple whose home I am selling! This home was not large but did have a spacious floor plan with vaulted ceilings. I had to side step in, facing one way, trying not to touch the dusty man-made additional interior walls compiled with book shelves, boxes, and fragile trinkets. Once I managed to get through, I walked into a large living area with a 20 foot vaulted ceiling, but it was a challenge to enjoy the space because of all the stuff. This is when I told them the truth. The clutter had to go! This is a tough step for some because they are emotionally attached. If this happens, explain that buyers prefer places that are not personalized.

For this seller, I was willing to help pre-pack them, and they wanted to move. During the decisions around what to keep and what to pack, I told the sellers to choose a few pieces of furniture they use. The husband chose his reclining brown leather chair and the wife chose her burgundy velvet chaise sofa. "Now, the rest of the things we are going to pre-move into a pod/self storage that comes to your house. It's easy." They were totally on board. With their help and the help of a stager, we manipulated the remaining furniture pieces, rearranged wall hangings, and decorated the kitchen and bathrooms. That house looked so amazing when it went on the market. The few pieces that we kept really showed off the home.

Now that the house was in selling condition, it was photo time. Potential buyers want to see photos. Over 90 percent of home buyers start their home search on the internet. When taking pictures, take into consideration the buyer is looking for something exciting in the photo to capture their eye, such as an amazing sunset view, an iron front, grape vines in back of the property, a grand kitchen, spa-like bathrooms, a three-car garage, a crystal blue pool, an aerial view, or even a floor plan. My priority is to upload as many quality photographs as possible to promote all the superior points and amenities of the property accompanied by descriptive text.

Once the house is decorated and the photos have been taken it is now time to market the property. It is important to get the attention of as many buyers as conceivable. I advertise on as many websites as possible. I advertise on many websites to increase the home's exposure. This opens the buying pool. Remember, it just takes one buyer. I try to post showing availabilities, so buyers may schedule their time around a clear schedule. Being flexible and making the home available is important. I want buyers through or how else are they going to know this is the house for them?

Lastly and most importantly is the pricing of the home. When pricing a home, I look at the comparative home sold prices in the area and how the "for sale" house compares. I take into consideration the size of the home, lot size, location, updates and amenities.

I run an internet search of all available homes in the area or zip code and look at the pricing to see if I can slot the "for sale" house. Slotting is placing your home intentionally in a certain order in the list. For example, if you have five very similar homes on the market, with two priced at $520,000; one priced at $515,000; one priced at $512,000 and one home priced at $500,000; I would strategically list the home at $513,000.

I would choose to price the home more expensively than the least expensive home and competitive with the others. I like to price a home within a few thousand dollars of the median but not the most expensive. Sometimes I do the math for my client that if they do not price it correctly the first time, then their property will get stale at the high price, and accrue more days on the market. More days on the market mean the seller is still paying for the property, the mortgage, insurance, taxes and homeowner's dues if applicable. So, if an offer comes in at $510,000 that would be a great price because it is the median price between $500,000 and $520,000.

Remember the couple seeking to move? They ended up with a ratified offer in 12 days on the market and received more than the list price. Success!

So remember these three tips when selling a house:

- de-clutter the property,

- market the property with numerous photos on many websites and make the property accessible to potential buyers, and

- price the property correctly the first time, don't let your house become stale.

In my business, I am always focused on obtaining the highest price for my sellers' in the shortest amount of time with the highest quality customer service and experience.

Happy selling.

ABOUT THE AUTHOR – Rebecca Selden

Since 2005, Rebecca Selden has sold real estate in an amazing part of the world, the San Francisco Bay Area. She works with a very successful privately-owned firm, Alain Pinel Realtors. In 2011, the APR company ranked in the top 10 for sales volume in the nation. Additionally, Rebecca has had her own hair design business for more than two decades. It has allowed her to expand visibility, master excellent customer service, provide honest feedback and built a loyal client following. It's been one resource for her client base.

Rebecca is a proud single mother of two athletic pre-teen sons. She is an active supporter of their school and sports activities; she participates in the community. Rebecca, a member of Soroptimist International, volunteers to help underprivileged women and children. As a native Californian, she has the knowledge to provide information to local and relocating families. She is always available by email at Rebecca@apr.com or by phone at 408.510.0855.

CHAPTER 15

The Buzz of the Right Price

By Erica Glessing

The dad walked in clutching a Craigslist ad I had posted at 9:30 p.m. the evening before. He brought two grown children through the house in Sunnyvale, California, and then walked through again, and then came back with a few more relatives.

On a fluke, I held this house open 12 hours after I posted it on the Multiple Listing Service, flying in the face of the standard home-selling practice in Sunnyvale at the time. The agents who sell in Sunnyvale would typically post on the MLS on a Tuesday, hold the home open for brokers on Thursday, then hold open houses Saturday and Sunday and cross their fingers for offers the following Tuesday.

This particular weekend in April was after Easter and before May, and the Saturday dawned so beautifully that I could not help but ask myself if I should change my plans. Instead of going with the norm, I popped the home on the market and it went pending before the broker's tour was held. In fact, by the time the "For Sale" sign was installed, before the scheduled broker's tour, I placed a "Pending" rider on it.

It sounds like luck, and if I hadn't experienced a dozen fast home sales that went effortlessly, I might attribute the results to luck. Behind the scenes, it went differently.

The price was set lower than the seller's original idea. This home was on a street where very few people sell! It is a very well-tended street. The market was declining, so it was a challenge to price in the way that I like to price. We priced at $618,000 when the sellers were originally thinking about $650,000. We looked at closed sold prices; and current competition for homes for sale. Nothing like this home was sold recently nearby, and the floor plan was unique. So, nothing was a perfect match for an easy sale price. We focused on what was possible given the current information available.

The home was cleaned from top to bottom! When the first stager came in, she said "I'm sorry you have to sell such a dog." Needless to say, she was not hired to stage this property. The next stager came in and fell in love with a few of the home's original attributes. It had custom kitchen cabinetry with lots of nooks and crannies for wine and baking sheets. There was a round window that faced the front yard, where the stager placed a simple vase with one decorative silk flower.

The hardwood floors were cleaned until they gleamed

and the bedrooms were left empty. The floor plan was quite unusual, with an added-on master bedroom in the back and a master bedroom in the front of the home.

When the buyers found the home on Sunday – clutching the ad that ran on the internet for the first time late Saturday night – it was the floor plan and the round window that ultimately sold them on the property. The son could occupy the back half of the home and the daughter would take the front of the home. The dad liked the quiet, safe street and the nice neighborhood. They offered under asking but it was very close, and the sellers accepted on a counter-offer.

The price generated the buzz, but the other pieces all had to fall into place for the home sale to work!

In another sale in Evergreen, a lovely hillside area of San Jose with good schools, I met with a divorcing couple who had to sell. The couple was fixated on the number $875,000 for their large, well-maintained and meticulously clean home.

Right at the same time the sellers were preparing to list their home for sale, a home with the same general lot size, floor plan and number of bedrooms and baths went up for sale about a block away on the same street. It was perfectly timed for the sellers to gather real-time data. The home was listed for $850,000 and when it went "pending," I was able to get good information from the listing agent. He received four offers and all were under asking. The price his sellers accepted was $845,000. Sometimes a real estate agent won't share the specifics, but will say "it sold within three percent of asking," or "the offers came in under" or "over" asking. So, you can't always get complete data but you can, if you ask, you can frequently receive some relevant data. Bingo! A few days after this neighboring home sold for $845,000, my sellers listed for $838,000.

The open house was a trample party with dozens and dozens of visitors. The sellers were motivated to get the best price, and spent time clearing clutter and pre-moving furniture out so the rooms looked spacious and welcoming. Offers came in and the sold price was $850,000.

I like to talk a nearby agent into sharing information on the pending price for a home with a similar floor plan and similar condition. When I can find out what buyers are offering, I believe I have a perfect tool for setting the right price on a home. Pending home sales are stronger indicators than closed, sold home sales when the home is a normal sale, because a pending price defines what buyers who are seeking homes right near yours are paying, right now! The second-best tool would be values on a recently sold home similar in characteristics.

I can see when a home sale is going to flow smoothly, from the very beginning. This is the key to a smooth home sale.

- The seller is perfectly clear they will sell. This is a firm clear commitment that will be communicated consciously and unconsciously throughout the home sale process.

- The seller expects the best, and allows the systems defined by the top people he or she hires go to work.

- If the price isn't sexy enough, no one is calling. Change the price if it is not generating excitement.

Couple a lower price with innovative marketing and strong home preparation. Look at what is working in your neighborhood, and then use all the tools you can find in this book to make sure the tools are working on your behalf.

I'll share one more story of a piece of land I sold during a time when vacant land was not selling at all. I was not the agent for this sale, I was the land owner. During the six-month period when my land was on the market, only two parcels of 24 parcels that were hanging out on the market ended up selling. This was in a rural and wild area of Santa Cruz County, close to Mt. Madonna County Park, and not close to anything else!

I priced the property fairly, and then I hired the very best land-selling agent for the region. This guy knows every parcel in the county and beyond! He has a map in his office with the parcels pinned and noted and his expertise runs miles and generations deep.

I offered a full commission (10 percent for vacant land) when some sellers were offering three percent per side or five percent total. I felt the 10 percent gave my agent and buyer agents a little bit of incentive to like and show my property more than the other properties. To see my property, the buyer's agent has to connect with my agent, and the listing agent has to take them two hours into the wilderness through four locked gates! We received one offer, all cash, full price, within four months, and we were done. I hired the best, paid him well, and felt good about the process because we were able to move on.

When you are ready to sell your house, or help your client sell their house, get very clear on the outcome. Have a clear outcome in mind and stick to this vision as you navigate all the decisions that come your way.

ABOUT THE AUTHOR – Erica Glessing

Erica Glessing is an author, real estate investment expert, motivational speaker, and the editor and co-publisher of "Sell Your House Fast for the Right Price." Her other books are "Prospect When You Are Happy," published in 2007, and "Happiness Quotations" published in 2011.

Her Facebook fan page www.Facebook.com/HappinessQuotations is well loved by more than 13,000 followers.

Erica became a top five percent Silicon Valley real estate agent the second year in business in the mid-2000s. She invests in rental properties with the help of the best agents she can find in the areas where she wishes to invest. Erica is the mom of three lovely children and a fabulous Tennessee Walking Horse named Dakotah. You can keep track of Erica's professional adventures at www.EricaGlessing.com.

SECTION IV

MARKETING INNOVATIONS...

CHAPTER 16

Selling the Unsellable House

By Jae Kim

Let's start with the basic elements of real estate. There are four aspects to consider when selling your home: Marketing, price, location and condition.

Marketing: Beating the odds in a neighborhood

One of our offices is located next door to a technology company. One of the managers from the company came over one day to our office and asked to talk with the broker. I asked the manager to sit down in the conference room for the usual new client meeting. I could immediately tell that he's the type to ask for a manager or broker because he believed he could have some room to negotiate by going this route.

His name was Michael and he had a home that he was interested in selling with us. He had heard about our office and he liked our reputation, through some of his friends and neighbors. He explained that he had already moved out into a larger home and was considering renting or selling his home. He was seeking advice in today's market. He wanted to sell, but he felt he may have to rent if the market was too difficult. After explaining his circumstances, he leaned back in his chair, crossed his arms and asked his first questions "So why should I go with you? What do you do that's so different than the other companies in town?"

I told Michael that the real estate market has changed drastically in the past few years and that, "there are two different parties to which you have to market. It's not as simple as attracting a buyer for your home anymore. That's just half the challenge to marketing properly in today's environment." I went on to explain to Michael that today's modern technology has made it so that virtually anyone can find a home if they have a computer and internet access. I explained to him, "the little known, surprising fact in today's market where over 90 percent of buyers begin their search online, is that over 90 percent of the people who buy a home STILL use a real estate agent to purchase a property." I told him that we market effectively to both buyers and other cooperating real estate agents to maximize his potential to sell his home.

Since Michael was in the technical field and was looking for straightforward answers, I gave him the detail he sought in such a way that he was receptive to it. I told him, "there are over 2,700 email addresses in our local Multiple Listing Service system. If you think that each of those agents is just waiting for your home to come on the market, you are mistaken. Like everyone else in today's world, they're multi-tasking and juggling every hour of the day." I clarified to him that I send an email out to everyone in the MLS using our company's exclusive contact management program, called PromoShop (which is powered by www.SharperAgent.com). Months earlier, we manually pulled every single email in our local MLS and converted that Excel file into a .csv file that is recognized by the Promoshop program. So, rather than hoping the agents in our MLS will conduct the correct search to find his listed home for their buyer clients, I drop an informative flyer providing the price and property details right into every agent's inbox the day I put the home on the market.

Additionally, I explained that I blog about the home in such a fashion that it leverages what Google, Yahoo and the other search engines like to see in online content to get their home to the first page of the respective searches using certain key terms. I reviewed with Michael a few examples of recent listings, including one listing entered that morning that actively came up on the first page of the online searches by the name of the neighborhood/subdivision. When he saw those listings show up because of the blogs on www.jaekimhomes.com, www.ExitRES.com, www.Trulia.com, www.Wordpress.com, www.ActiveRain.com, and a few other sites, he understood the power of real-time online marketing.

Having clearly satisfied Michael's need to know about the modern marketing that I do in addition to the traditional methods of marketing, he moved on to his next phase of questioning.

He asked, "Will you do a discount commission?" I simply smiled and replied "no." I explained to him that the circumstances surrounding his home and the competition in his area would make having a discount listing against his best interests. He then proceeded to ask, "What percentage will you charge to sell our home?" Since I could tell he was still in an aggressive mood where he believed someone had to lose for him to win, I went with the answer that usually disarms someone in this situation. I answered quite simply "that depends." And then I sat awaiting his response. He leaned forward and asked, "What do you mean by that?" Thus began the lesson on using commission as a marketing tool.

Because of the area his home was located in Northeast Columbia, he had strong competition from new construction, as well as foreclosures. I told him that he should list his home with a bonus or at least an extra percent to the buyer's agent in commission. Well, you would have thought I told him that the nation just started using $3 bills. It was clear that he adamantly opposed the idea.

He asked, "Why in the world would I pay MORE to sell my home?" I told Michael, "You have to remember that real estate agents are independent contractors and are not paid to do hourly or salaried work. They simply hang their license with their companies. Each agent conducts business on their own, within the company's guidelines, and they only make money when they help clients buy or sell properties. In our area, the average agent will sell between 4-7 homes in any given year.

That's not a lot of homes so each sale is very important to them." I could tell I had his attention because he seemed to be a little more relaxed and was actively listening. To help him understand it a little clearer, I asked him to role play with me for a moment.

I used my example of painting a room. I told Michael, "Imagine you're a painting contractor and I've asked you to come by to give me a quote. After I hear your recommendation on the paint color, paint type and trim paint, I decide to allow you to paint one of my two bedrooms. Now, here's the catch, I really only want one room painted. I'll pay you $100 to paint the room on the right and $150 to paint the room on the left, but you're only allowed to paint just one room." I then went on to tell him, "I'll let YOU choose which room to paint." He says, "Well, of course, I'd pick the $150 room on the left." I said, "Precisely! Now I am simply leveraging the fact that people are struggling to make ends meet in this market, including agents, and using buyer's agent commission as a tool to attract more attention is simply using what's available to you, to your advantage."

Michael decided that he liked what he heard and signed the listing contract with me. I took the usual wide-angle pictures, created the virtual tour, put up the sign, and then started the non-traditional marketing efforts. On the 10th day on the market, we received our first offer. Since we had another offer coming in, we leveraged that first offer for a higher price.

Needless to say, Michael was ecstatic! After a brief negotiating session, we ended up selling the home to that buyer for $2000 over asking price on a $115,000 home.

Here is where it got fun. Michael recommended that one of his neighbors, Thomas, contact me to do the same for him. I sat down with Thomas to explain what we did and how we did it and he agreed that I should sell his home as well. He signed on with me immediately. On the 12th day on the market, I received a call from someone who saw the new listing in one of our blogs. Luckily, they had already driven through the neighborhood to check out the home and the surrounding area. I showed the military transferee and his wife the home and we wrote the contract that same day with a full price offer. I recently sold a third home in Michael's old neighborhood about seven homes away for full price.

Here is what it looked like when you compared my three sales with the rest of the activity in the same neighborhood...

• The three homes I sold averaged 100.56 percent of their final listing price and had an average sale price of $118,900.

• In the same time frame of March 2011 to March 2012 in the same neighborhood, eight other properties sold. They sold at 87.02 percent of their final listing price and had an average sale price of $76,918.

Marketing: Selling the "Unsellable" Home

This is about a home that the seller and everyone in the neighborhood thought would NEVER sell. It was a new construction home in an upscale, golf course community neighborhood, Chickasaw Woods. The home had four stories which included a walk-out basement, with the main level and upstairs very traditionally set and tailored to fit in with the rest of the neighborhood.

The interesting part was the downstairs led to another level that had two full bedrooms, each with it's own bathroom, and a family room that's about the size of a garage. Walk down one more level to the walk-out basement and you find a wine cellar, a den with a stacked stone fireplace, a wet bar, a play room set up for a pool table and 180 degree views of the golf course. It reminded me of a retreat you'd find in the mountains of Colorado on the edge of a ski resort. There are windows along the entire back of the home to maximize the views of the back yard and golf course.

As a new construction home, it was first put on the market with the on-site agent starting on February 2007, and stayed on for just over 500 days. The builder who finished the home then decided to become a real estate agent (thinking it would be easier). He personally took over the listing in July 2008 and tried to sell the upscale home himself with simple exposure in the MLS and a sign in the yard. Sadly, the builder got behind on his payments for the home and the bank repossessed it. The bank then re-listed the home with the on-site agent's firm in June 2009. Some marketing was done through the local real estate magazine and the MLS, but again it was the usual traditional marketing. After over 480 days on the market, the bank decided they needed to go with someone else.

This brand new home was then re-listed by the largest independent brokerage in Greater Columbia. After just under nine months on the market, again with very minimal marketing besides the traditional methods, it was withdrawn from the market.

A few years before, I had lunch with a rising star agent, Richard, with another local real estate company. Richard wanted to get some inside information on what it took to become a top-producing agent. I was surprised and flattered when he called me and we had a great lunch at Olive Garden and soon we became good friends in the business. Well, come to find out, he had a great working relationship with the bank that owned that large new house, and he recommended me to help them sell this home. Next thing you know, I get a call from Richard and he tells me that he's going to have Milton, the asset manager at the bank, call me about marketing and advertising some distressed properties.

Up to now, I've been working for about a year straight trying to get some REO (real estate owned) properties from banks. I've made the usual round of calls to local banks, submitted applications to national banks, contacted asset managers with top REO companies, etc... No luck landing a nice company with the exception of a few small one-listing companies. Well, Milton called me early one Monday morning and introduced himself. He tells me that he wants to begin a relationship and that he will let me try my hand at the "challenging" listings to prove myself. Naturally, I tell him that I'm up to the challenge.

When he tells me that it's 112 Chickasaw Lane, I can feel this sudden weight in the middle of my stomach. It wasn't necessarily nausea, but more like a bowling ball that kept me from being able to move. At the same time, I feel a release of just a tiny bit of sweat out of every single pore on my entire body. I knew that this would be one of the most challenging listings I'd ever worked!

What you need to know is that I drive past this "challenging" home every day. This is not a unique property to me, as I've personally shown it no less than 10 times with buyers and investors. I've watched it as the listings went up on the MLS and then expired with all the previous agents. I've watched my kids get rezoned for 3 different schools in the time that I've seen this home for sale. When Milton asked if I knew about it, I had to contain myself and reply with a simple, "Yes, I've seen it on the market recently." Milton went on to say, "Well, if you can get this one sold, you're going to be my hero." By the conviction in his voice, I could tell he really meant it.

As is my usual approach to a new listing, I conducted a comparative marketing analysis to see what the home would sell at in today's market. Once we agreed on a price of $480,000, it was time to chart the right marketing path for the challenging home. Because this home had been on the market for so much time already, with a few of the other large firms in the area, I know that exposure with the local real estate public did not have to be my primary focus. Nearly EVERYONE knew it had been for sale. I knew that I needed to reach the general public, especially those who knew this neighborhood extremely well and those from out of town.

I started out with a postcard blast to the neighborhood and the surrounding neighborhoods. That immediately informed all the previously interested parties that the home was back on the market with an updated price. Later, I found out that it was through the use of postcards we would land our first offer. I then emailed out to our 2700+ MLS emails that I had in my mass email program, PromoShop, so that all the agents in the Greater Metro area of Columbia would know it was again on the market.

As my next marketing piece, I had a blog created that highlighted the strong points of our listing, most notably the lowered price and location on the golf course. Within the first week, Margaret, an agent with a local firm, made contact and said, "I have a buyer who was interested in the house from the last time it was listed and he just saw a marketing piece indicating that it was available again."

During the same time, I was also flooded with emails requesting more information about the home from my website, the brokerage website, Zillow.com, Trulia.com and a few other real estate sites. One email stood out. It was from a buyer named Phyllis who just happened to catch it while surfing the web. She told me, "I have parents living in town and I have a large family so I need a larger home than what is available in the general market." I arranged to meet Phyllis and her family at the home to see if our listing would in fact work for her. But, before I could show it to her, an offer came in from Margaret.

As a courtesy, I contacted Phyllis about the offer. Phyllis replied "Jae, I'm not interested in a bidding war so I'll wait to see if it comes available again." Still, I encouraged her by saying, "in today's market, you have to understand that roughly 25 to 35 percent of deals fall through before closing so it's in your best interest to make an offer on this home." Well, that was enough to get her to see the home. Interestingly, it was her mother, Hazel, who I showed it to first because Phyllis lived out of town. When Phyllis said her mother lived close, she meant REALLY close. Hazel was less than three miles away and come to find out she desperately wants her daughter's family to live close to her.

Later that night, Hazel delivered the news to Phyllis that this was the home for her. I set up another meeting with her family and this time, everyone, I mean EVERYONE, shows up. When you have three full SUVs pull up, you know it's going to be a fun time. Well, Phyllis loved the home just as much as Hazel said she would. Nate, her husband, who is into having a place for his stuff, liked the fact that it has "Man Cave" potential. It's a perfect fit for them and their growing family. We wrote the offer that night. I submitted it to Milton as a nicely priced backup offer. Milton immediately accepted the backup contract the following morning.

Closing time is coming up for the first offer with Margaret and the buyer is not supplying the details needed in order to close. My messages to Margaret go unanswered, always a bad sign just before closing. Needless to say and not too surprisingly, it didn't close. Offer #2 then became the primary contract and, oh boy was Phyllis excited! She was so excited that we scheduled another viewing of the property that day just so she could check out the rooms for the placement of her existing furniture. I love when the buyers do that! We had the occasional hiccup with lending and appraiser issues, but we ended up closing well before the contract close date.

After closing, Nate carried Phyllis in his arms through the front door and they were unbelievably excited, as only new homeowners could be. Little did we know that our unsellable house had one more surprise in store. Phyllis turned the HVAC unit on to warm the home up just a little. Oddly, the home's temperatures just wouldn't adjust to a comfortable level. Nate, equally puzzled, checked to see what was going on and tried out another unit.

At this point, I had driven down the street basking in the warmth of that great feeling you get when you close a tough deal. As I turned at the end of the street to leave, I saw Nate waving his arms frantically. Naturally, I drove back up to the home to see what was going on. It seems while we were at the attorney's office finalizing this closing, some local thieves decided that the HVAC units were just too easy to pass up, just sitting there looking all pretty and new. All that we found were cut-off lines going into the home. Well, the good news is that the insurance covered the replacement units and the bank was more than happy to help to coordinate the work. Thus, we sold the unsellable home.

Location

Unless you can move your home, this is a category with little margin for discussion. Things like schools, proximity to highways, shopping and the growth rate of the area will factor into the value placed on location.

Setting the Right Price

This is the market's determination of what your home is worth today. This is NOT what your neighbor thinks it is worth. It is NOT what your county tax assessor says it is worth. It is worth whatever a buyer is willing to pay for it TODAY. 2006 prices simply do not apply. If you have an appraisal older than six months (or three months in a fast-changing market), then you need more current information. You can hire an appraiser with the sole purpose of determining value or you can have an experienced agent conduct a CMA (comparative market analysis) or a BPO (broker price opinion). For most situations, a CMA by an experienced agent will be sufficient. The most recent sales will indicate what today's buyer believes is a good market value for your home. It doesn't matter what price the next door neighbor has listed her home. Listed homes don't determine today's value. Recently sold homes determine true market value.

Getting the Home into Top Condition

This is a shared responsibility. The agent will need to provide guidance on what today's buyer expects to see in a home that is comparable to your home. I recommend that you want to be better than your competition, for obvious reasons. The homeowner's responsibility is to get the house in tip-top shape to help the prospective buyer fall in love with your home.

If the agent says your carpet needs to be replaced, replace it. If they say the home needs to be caulked and painted, then spend the extra time, money and effort to get it done. Deferred maintenance items should be resolved to maintain your home's top value.

ABOUT THE AUTHOR – *Jae Kim*

 Jae Kim is a Georgia Tech graduate with a degree in Mechanical Engineering. He worked for 12 years in engineering, distribution and manufacturing management with companies like www.Amazon.com, Target, Mobil Chemical, W.R. Grace , and QVC.

Jae has listed over 500 properties and $50 million in sales since 2005. He has extensive experience in the real estate industry from past purchases and sales (renovations, foreclosures, short sales, duplexes, quads, apartments, commercial property, resort land). He leverages his experience to help his clients and their needs. He has extensive experience in relocations, military transfers, & investments. He has been in 38 states (and counting) and has lived in Georgia, Alabama, Kentucky, South Carolina, and North Carolina after growing up in Florida.

Jae began his real estate career with Coldwell Banker in Camden, SC. He had his first full year in 2005. Jae moved to RE/MAX in 2007 and started his first team. In 2008, Jae became a broker and his team maintained an average of 40 listings with an average price of $200,000. In 2009, Jae received the prestigious CRS® designation, placing him in the top 4 percent of all real estate sales agents nationwide. In May 2009, EXIT Real Estate Solutions, opened its doors to the public with Jae Kim as the Owner and Broker-in-Charge. In 2010, Jae received the ABR®(Accredited Buyer's Representative) and SFR® (Short Sales and Foreclosure Resource) designations. In February 2012, the second office for EXIT Real Estate Solutions, this one in Irmo, SC opened for business. Jae remains in the top 1 percent of agents in the Greater Columbia area.

Contact Jae Kim here:

www.JaeKimHomes.com

CHAPTER 17

The Real Estate Game Plan

By Phyllis Harb

Prior to selling real estate I worked in the mortgage banking business. My last position was vice president overseeing the loan processing, appraisal and funding departments for the mortgage banking division of Sterling Bank. I had many functions but one of my most interesting tasks was to write a policy and procedure manual for the loan processing department. It was very detailed and a lot of fun.

I left the mortgage banking business and began selling real estate in 1989. During my first few months as a Realtor® the market plummeted. I could not have asked for better on the job training. No longer did a real estate agent place a for sale sign in the ground and collect offers. The real estate climate had changed, and I had the opportunity to learn from it.

What I learned during the 1990s downturn:

- Buyers were frightened
- There were lots of foreclosures and few short sales
- Banks were more aggressive with lending; especially with their foreclosures (special/more lenient financing was readily available when purchasing their foreclosures)

Target marketing was a key aspect of a listing agent's success in selling a home in this downturn:

- Who was the likely buyer?
- Where would we find them? Print advertising, employee bulletin boards?
- Networking with other real estate agents… (This was before the advent of the internet, which was a game changer)

Many real estate agents survived the downturn and we plunged into the heady days of our heated real estate market during the new millennium. Homes selling for as much as $100,000 over asking price were not the exception in my Los Angeles market, but often the norm.

But there is one important aspect to remember about real estate: It goes up and it goes down. And in 2006 it began its downward descent.

So what does it take to sell your home in today's real estate climate? A plan; I developed the Real Estate

Game Plan. My home seller's game plan is surprisingly simple and it works in **any** real estate market.

Step 1: Meet with your Realtor® and review comparable sales and listings. Arrive at an asking price, sign listing contract.

Step 2: Each home seller has different needs and for those who wish to sell their home for the highest possible price, preparing their home for sale is a major factor in obtaining top dollar. As part of my marketing package I provide my clients with a complimentary home staging consultation. Should you repaint? And if so which color? Does furniture need to be rearranged? The way we live in a home and the way we showcase it for sale are completely different.

Step 3: Once any desired staging is completed and the home is prepped for sale, I send a professional photographer to take high resolution photos of my listings. A home seller's first showing will be online – the internet. We want the buyer to like what they see and to call to schedule an appointment for a personal preview.

Step 4: Now that we have professional photos, the real marketing campaign can begin. Coming soon advertising is in place.

Step 5: We are approaching our first open house, the Broker's Caravan day. This is the designated day when local Realtors® preview the new listings. We have input the listing into the Multiple Listing Service (MLS) and are just waiting for showings. Circumstances can vary;

often your home will be in the MLS for a few days with no showings allowed until caravan day.

Step 6: Review, negotiate offers and open escrow.

Step 7: Home successfully closed.

Success story:

Each home seller has a different set of priorities. Several years ago a potential home seller contacted my office in the fall. He wanted to sell his home in the spring. His employer was relocating him and his wife was reluctant to leave her home, the neighborhood and her family. His priority was to sell the home with the least disruption to his wife and children.

We decided that the best way for him to keep everyone happy was to send his family on a one week cruise during Spring Break and I had that week to market, show and sell their home.

We applied my Real Estate Game Plan. The key factor was that this client contacted me early in the selling process. His wife met with the stager and we leisurely made repairs and changes. The photographer took photos, we began our marketing campaign. The day his family departed on their Mexican Riviera cruise we came on the market and when the family returned we accepted an offer, opened escrow and in five weeks closed.

I am a believer of timing when a new listing comes on the market, and the onset of spring break when a lot of home buyers and real estate agents are out of town is not ideal. But this home seller's priority was to have minimal family disruption. Although with our real estate game plan, we were able to sell his home for over the asking price, his primary concern was keeping peace in the family. Fortunately we were able to meet all of his goals.

Here is my advice for selling your home quickly at the highest possible price:

After a buyer views your home online, they may do a quick drive by to determine if it's a home they want to further pursue. What are they going to see when they drive by your home? **Here are my top ten curb appeal tips:**

1. Trim shrubs and trees in the front yard; a home buyer should be able to see your home's architectural features (that beautiful picture window). Tidy up your yard; put away hoses, trash cans, etc.

2. Remove the screen door (if any) dress up the front porch with a plant (if room), wash your windows and your screens.

3. If the mailbox is visible from the curb, ensure that it is attractive.

4. Repaint any peeling trim or exterior paint. Prior to selecting paint colors, consult with your Realtor® or home stager for color selection.

5. Define the approach: Add a stone walkway or path leading to the house, or define with plants or flowers.

6. Ensure any automatic lights along the house and walkways light as it gets dark.

7. When visible from the street, replace your tired looking garage door with a new one. Remember to keep the door style in tune with your home's architectural style.

8. How does the driveway look? Is it cracked? If so consider repair or resurface.

9. Add details such as shutters, decorative moldings. Make boring windows come alive and (depending on your homes style) define the architecture of your house with shutters or ironwork.

10. Last suggestion: Imagine the real estate agent at your front door fumbling with the lock box; the home buyer is looking at your neighborhood, what do they see? Is there trash in the street? Is the neighbor's lawn overgrown? Look around and discuss with your real estate agent how you can increase your home's curb appeal.

Success story:

Earlier this year, I met with a potential home seller. He and his family were relocating. They wanted to sell their home, close escrow, rent back their home until the kids got out of school and pay cash for a new home out of state.

They met with my home stager, repainted the interior, replaced the carpet in the bathrooms with vinyl, refinished hardwood floors, rearranged furniture, and a few more tasks. As they met with me early in the selling process they had a couple of months to complete these tasks. Their priority was to sell their home for the highest possible price and they insisted on renting back the home in order to allow their children to complete the school year.

Again, the game plan worked beautifully! Once their home was prepped for sale, we began advertising. After the front was spruced up, we placed a for sale sign in the ground. After the first week of open houses we reviewed offers, accepted one, and opened escrow. We negotiated the seller rent back and the seller had the cash to purchase his out of state home without financing.

Final advice, discuss with your real estate agent your priorities: price, convenience, maximizing profit etc. and then develop a winning game plan to meet your real estate needs.

ABOUT THE AUTHOR – Phyllis Harb

Phyllis Harb's expertise, enthusiasm, and passion for excellence have resulted in happy clients and an amazing track-record in real estate sales. Cited as a "Super Agent" by Los Angeles Magazine, Phyllis offers over 25 years of combined real estate and mortgage banking experience. Having sold in excess of 1000 homes, Harb is recognized as one of the premier Realtors® in LA, ranking among the top 5 percent of real estate professionals nationally.

She is well known for her strong negotiating skills, keen marketing strategies and her use of the latest technologies. Learn more about Phyllis by visiting her @ www.RealtorHarb.com and her highly acclaimed Los Angeles real estate blog at www.LAreBlog.com.

Contact Phyllis @ Phyllis@RealtorHarb.com or (818) 790-7325.

CHAPTER 18

Making All the Right Moves

By Eric Pearson

The New Way to Sell a Home

Only 12 percent of real estate agents are under the age of 40. When I meet with a seller to talk about selling his or her home, I am usually half the age of my client. Needless to say, when I got into the business at 25 years of age, I had to do my due diligence to find out what exactly sells a home in today's market so that I could gain the trust of my clients.

From the beginning, I have always worked off of the theory that the new way to sell a home is actually still the old way. When pricing a home, go back to basics and be up front with the seller from the start. Unrealistic expectations yield unrealistic results, and vice versa.

Step One: Price a home appropriately to sell for top dollar

Pricing in my mind is an art form. Pricing is by the far the most important talk you will have with a seller. The price tag should come down to what the home is worth in the current market, factoring in supply and demand. The first three weeks the home is on the market are critical. That is when most traffic comes through the home. Price it wrong and you will end up chasing the market, and getting less for your property than if you listed correctly in the beginning. My favorite objections when reviewing pricing with a client are:

· Well, I paid XXX for it, so I want to sell if for YYY...

· My neighbor was telling me the other day that our homes are worth...

· I have a friend who did real estate for a while and she was telling me I could get...

· I really don't have to sell, so let's price it at...

The market has either appreciated or depreciated since you bought the home, so the price that was paid has just about nothing to do with the current market value. The real question is do you *want* to sell your home?

The most important part of being an agent is always being honest and up front, even through the most difficult of discussions. Allowing someone to overprice the home will usually lead to a lower sales price. Once a listing becomes stale, price reductions have very little effect on getting traffic of potential buyers through a home. Do you want to buy stale bread even if it's half priced?

I have found that being open, honest and backing up pricing with detailed market information including comparable listings, comparable sales data, and square footage cost comparisons is the best way to gain the trust of the seller from the initial meeting.

A Little Known Secret about Pricing!

Buyers typically search in $50,000 increments. So if a detailed pricing analysis shows your property being worth $350,000, then you should list at $350,000. While $349,900 is much more appealing to the eye, at $350,000 your property will appear for a buyer searching for homes between $300,000 and $350,000, and also for a buyer searching between $350,000 and $400,000. You just doubled the number of buyers who will come through your home on a $100 price adjustment. On the other hand, if you home is worth $320,000 then it is fine to list at $319,900 – it simply appears more attractive and will not affect the number of people who will see your home.

One online pricing strategy I use that works extremely effective is through the Zillow Premier Agent Program. I can market up to six of your listings with a Zillow Special Offer, typically an incentive towards the buyer's closing costs. When a Special Offer is placed on a listing, that listing shows up first not once ... but EVERY TIME a buyer searches for a home in that zip code or city!

I just finished a successful sale with a client where all these pricing strategies played an important role in receiving multiple offers and the full list price in just six days on market. She was extremely stressed out after a bad experience with a popular discount broker. She was settling on a new construction home in four weeks, and she was in the middle of finals for her MBA. She called me after I put an "under contract" sign on my listing up the street and very emotionally said to me, "Eric, I need help!" I met with her and discussed her situation in detail.

The strategy was simple – we would price at $350,000, place a Zillow Special Offer on the property, market aggressively on the internet and I said, "I will be with you every step of the way." We settled just 17 days later! She passed her finals and she is now enjoying her new home stress-free.

Step Two: The home should be in good condition and show well

It is often said that buyers make up their mind within eight seconds as to whether or not they are interested in a property. With that being said, would you think twice about buying a car from a dealership if the car was filled with trash, sippy cups, and stains? Why would someone want to make an even bigger investment on a home that doesn't show well?

When full staging is not an option, little changes go a long way. Suggest shopping for accessories that work. Even a small thing like fresh towels in bathrooms can make a world of difference. The owners should de-clutter. Keep animals at bay when possible. Little changes can make the difference between listing a home that is viewed as needing work, to selling a home that is move-in ready. Listing a home is a team project, and all parties should enter the contract with the agreement that this is a team deal. Is it worth making the bed to sell your home? Yes!

The first listing that came my way was a house in an affluent area that was surrounded by acreage and serenity in the Washington Metro area. It was extremely rare. However, the deck was tired, old, filled with leaves, and had rotten furniture. As a new agent, I rolled up my sleeves, power-washed the deck, swept it, and borrowed a few accessories to turn the deck into an outdoor oasis within hours. Both the dining room and the living room were being used as reading areas and I immediately saw how buyers would think there was no dining room, so I hauled a table to the house and staged one area for dining. A few of the bedrooms were cluttered and looked like multipurpose rooms. Without furniture or a budget, I improvised. I tipped over a bookcase, laying it face down, and put a mattress on top resulting in an instant clutter-free bedroom. Little changes go a long way. This resulted in a sale within five days, a happy client, and a smashing start for my newborn business.

Step Three: Marketing your home

Here's where I tell you what sells a home for top dollar...the internet! Yes, I remain old-school in my pricing tactics and traditional in my wisdom, but I am where I am today because of the World Wide Web. As one of the x-generation, I was fully aware that the internet, social media, and online networking could facilitate a platform to skyrocket my business. Web-based services make it possible to connect with thousands and open up doors to market a home across political, economic, and geographic borders. The internet has completely changed the game of real estate. Having the awareness and ability to stay on top of current trends and tactics to sell a home is a must.

Today, buyers start their home search online. Few people today look for homes in the paper or attend open houses first, when wanting to make their purchase. They are searching on Homes.com, Zillow, Realtor.com, Trulia, Yahoo and other sites to find the home they want to buy. You can't simply be on these sites, you have to stand out! By having a premier agent relationship with these companies, your agent can literally have your home show up first every time someone searches in your zip code. Then your home is the center of attention to millions of buyers each and every day! Single property website, social media, QR codes, blogging, online classified advertising, pay-per click advertising, SEO strategies ... these are all great for business, and your agent should know how make your home visible to each and every potential home buyer.

Every listing I've had the opportunity and privilege to list, I've sold. I never know which exact marketing source is going to sell your home. What I do know is whether you are young, old, experienced, inexperienced, or anything in between – being successful in the real estate world all boils down to staying on top of market trends and technology, and coupling back-to-basics principles, honesty, hard work, and passion to be at the top of your game – for your client's sake and for your own livelihood.

ABOUT THE AUTHOR – *Eric Pearson*

At 25, Eric Pearson took a leap of faith – saying goodbye to his career in accounting and entered the world of real estate. As a former NCAA basketball team captain, he used his leadership skills, keen business sense, and superior customer service skills to take the market by storm. Eric proves how the proper use of social networking and an extensive marketing plan, combined with drive and hard work can quickly move new agents to the top of the game. His listings average over 99 percent of list and under 25 days on market – talk about selling homes FAST and for TOP DOLLAR. He is on track to complete over 100 transactions during his first full year (2012) as the face of E4Realty.

E4Realty is a real estate company partnered with RE/MAX Gateway located in Brambleton, VA. E4Realty is committed to providing the highest level of customer service, extending far past a successful settlement. With their extensive knowledge and experience in the Northern Virginia residential real estate market, you can depend on E4Realty to bring all aspects of your real estate transaction together. Their team of dedicated professionals has earned E4Realty its reputation for service excellence. Allow E4Realty to assist you in answering any questions regarding the home buying or selling process and their services.

Contact Eric Pearson at (540) 454-1551

www.e4realty.com, eric@e4realty.com

CHAPTER 19

Marketing is Sweeter in Miami Beach

By Kelly Charles with Louise O'Donnell

Tom and Karen are in love. They met on an internet dating site, and even though he lives in Minnesota and she lives in Utah, they have been working hard at creating a relationship together for the last five years. They wanted a place where they could spend time together and relax. They came to Miami, FL a few times and fell in love with the city so they decided that they would make an investment in their future.

When you are selling a home, it is vital to attract the right buyer. I have met many buyers in Miami, and I've come to learn many things about the city. I know that Miami is a special place, full of glamour, beaches and sunsets, glorious nightlife and laid-back culture. It's the kind of place that attracts dreamers and lovers. It's true that some of those dreams are flaky. I've been approached by tourists to take them on a guided tour of some of the most exclusive apartments in town, or by middle-aged ladies that want to put their jewelry down as a deposit on a place they fell in love with. As a Realtor®, I watch potential buyers carefully, and when I met Tom and Karen and heard their story, I thought it was sweet.

However, what really impressed me about them was what they already knew about the different neighborhoods in the city. With the connections to many different airlines at Miami International and the nearby Fort Lauderdale airports, Miami was also an accessible place for both of them. They had made their decision carefully and researched well. They knew the ballpark market prices for the type of apartment they wanted and they were able to show that they were good for the finance, which is great for me to know as a Realtor® .

For well-prepared buyers who know what they want and what they can and can't afford, like Tom and Karen, it's easy to find the perfect property. I was selling a cute little apartment in the Terra Beachside Villas complex on Collins Ave, which was right in their price range. I hadn't had it on my books for long. Lynda, the vendor, wanted a quick sale. I had shared a few nice cups of tea with Lynda. She was looking for a quick sale on the property so she could invest in a new business in the United Kingdom (UK). I enjoyed Lynda's company and was impressed by her china cups, but even more so by the apartment itself. It was a great two-story loft with a private roof deck, directly across from the beach in a quiet Mid-Beach location. This wonderful, true-Miami-style condo was completely move-in ready, with white porcelain floors and Italian leather furniture. It was exciting to bring Tom and Karen to the apartment. They looked at home there. They were effusive in their praise for the place, and were talking about hosting guests on their roof deck.

I find it so inspiring when I see people taking steps forward to making their dreams come true. It was a well-ordered and efficient sale process. The price was right for Tom and Karen and right for Lynda, who was free to move back to an exciting new business in England. I think it can be a mistake to set buyer and seller against each other. Sometimes there is just a great place to meet in the middle. Negotiations can be win-win, and in this case they definitely were!

Tom and Karen kept the apartment as a second home for a while, and they would spend time together there whenever they could. Eventually they decided that they wanted to make the move permanent, and now they are married and living in Miami full-time. Miami is a big city and there are jobs in many sectors, not just in tourism, cruises and hospitality that it is famous for! I see them around town from time to time, and I'm so pleased that things seem to be working out for them. This makes me remember that real estate is about going for what you want in life, and creating something new.

Talking of creativity, I want to tell you about Julian, an artist from Switzerland. He has been coming to Miami for every year for the last 10 years as a regular contributor to the Art Basel festival. Miami has a flourishing contemporary arts scene, the Art Basel festival being one of the many arts festivals that grace the city each year. The city is popular with contemporary artists, such as the well-known Brazilian pop artist Romero Britto.

Selling an apartment to an artist was an interesting challenge. Julian was looking for something well designed, well located for the beaches and the South Beach party scene and modestly priced.

Julian talked to me about being in love the city, especially at sunset when the sky moves through a particular range of pastels colors matched by the paints of the buildings in the Art Deco district. The architecture of the city is grand, bold and beautiful – revolutionary and contemporary from the 1930s onwards, with many new innovative buildings adding modern beauty to the skyline. I knew I could find something that Julian would find inspiring.

The developers of a complex called Arte City suffered due to timing, as the complex was completed in 2008. The Miami real estate market suffered quite a bit during the recent crash, and the original developers faced bankruptcy. A new company purchased the note from the bank and re-launched the project, by which time the Miami real estate market was recovering, buoyed in part by interest from international investors, like Julian who could benefit from a weak dollar. The new owners of Arte City needed to be realistic about the price that they could attain for their individual units. They released the units to the market slowly and carefully, to ensure that they achieved good cash flow.

Julian was delighted when I showed him a 2-bedroom unit in Arte City. The development ticked all the boxes regarding the price, design and location. The building is located right on the Mid-Beach/South Beach border, not far from the public beach and very close to the shopping, nightlife and arts hotspot that is Lincoln Road. A big plus for Julian was its proximity to key cultural resources such as the Miami City Ballet, the Bass Museum and the Miami Convention Center, that hosts the Art Basel festival! I negotiated a good deal for Julian for his home, as the seller had priced it right. He's in Europe at the moment working on projects and family business, and is looking for somebody to rent the property for a year. The rental market is typically very buoyant on Miami Beach, so a good quality build like this one will rent quickly at the right price. He's looking forward to coming across to Miami to be inspired in his stylish new home and the glamorous city that brings the world together.

ABOUT THE AUTHORS – *Kelly Charles with Louise O'Donnell*

Originally from the UK, Kelly Charles has earned a solid reputation with clients and fellow realtors® as an agent you will want to work with, and stay with for life! She prides herself on integrity, sophistication, honesty and intelligence (and has a great accent!)

Having traveled the globe, she lived on three continents before settling in her beach home in Miami. She has an infectious love of the city and enjoys working with overseas buyers realizing their dream in this tropical paradise. A graduate from the University of Southampton with a degree in Mathematics, she is always up-to-date with the real estate market and has been successful in buying and selling homes, even in tough economic climates. Prior to her blossoming career in real estate, she climbed the corporate ladder with British Airways, holding management positions in London, New York and Miami.

Kelly's story was written with help from Louise O' Donnell, who can help with your blog too! louise@urbanfaery.com.

You can contact Kelly Charles via her website: www.BritishMiamiRealtor.com

CHAPTER 20

But I Don't Want to Sell (and How to Let Go)

By Lisa Jordan Watts, PhD, ThD

But I Don't Want to Sell My House!

Moving? No choice? Having trouble letting go?

"We have lived in our home 20 years, raised our children here, and now my husband has been transferred 500 miles away." The voice on the other end of the phone was weary and stressed. I could tell she had been crying and this was a difficult experience for their family. Sometimes our choices feel like they may as well be no choices. This family had to relocate. Saying 'no' would mean throwing away a career of 25 years and all of the benefits, retirement and pension plans that went with it. Saying 'yes' is leaving all that is comfortable behind.

"We worked so hard to save the money we put down on our house a few years ago, now we are faced with a decision that

could mean throwing all of it out the window. Giving up our home is devastating, we love everything about it." This was a must-sell situation that became more urgent every month the house sat on the market. So far, this home owner had experienced no magic equation for a sale. Reducing the price again accelerated the negative slope of any hope of retaining what should have been their equity.

These two families shared the need to sell their home, but also the thought process of attachment. Attachment does not serve the seller! Like it or not, the brutal truth is that selling your property is a business transaction. It is not a great idea to do business with your emotions. There are no warm fuzzies in your bank account or the bottom line. It's hard to let go when we are too attached.

I know firsthand what it is like to have to relocate unwillingly or suddenly. And it has nothing to do with the 15 times I had to move, growing up, either. As a child I liked moving. My parents always enjoyed the process and my mom loved decorating her new home. That's it. *Home.*

Just a few years ago, on a fall afternoon, my small dog beside me, I was coming home from an afternoon walk. Clicking the turn signal and turning into my road, I noticed several vehicles stopped at the entrance, directing traffic. I thought perhaps it was emergency vehicles for a neighbor. When I turned into my road, my heart sank. Straight ahead I saw the smoke billowing out of the roof and firefighters all around my house. That's it. My *House.* Because 'Home 'was sitting beside me, 'Home' was my family, 20 minutes away at work and a few hours away at school. My 'home' was not burning, but my 'house' was. That house was full of things that made our home, but the hearts that brought those things to fruition are still here.

Divorce, death and believe it or not, losing your house all carry loss and loss must have time to grieve. So, try to be smart, realize you are going to grieve in the process of moving. Choose your real estate professional. Engage thoughts and possible solutions with them to balance your objectivity as you begin to plan your strategy for this business transaction. Discuss options, terms, absolute numbers, your preferences, and make the best realistic conclusion for your situation. Before you know it, you'll be looking forward to the move.

Remind yourself often that you are selling your house, not your home. Allow yourself and your family the opportunity to grieve. Share thoughts and ideas about leaving your current house; and most of all, share ideas about the ways you want to enjoy making your new home.

OK, let's break it down. Like anything else we are not crazy about doing, we have to accept some things as part of life. More particularly, life goes better when we are not in resistance to our life journey.

When letting go of your house is part of your life journey, give your house one more hug. It's the place where you raised your children, held countless family gatherings – dinners, reunions, birthdays, anniversaries and more. It's the place where you solved problems and shared secrets over the kitchen table late at night. The good news is that these are all going with you, to the new house you will make home. These are your memories, not your house.

Now let us look at new houses! Focusing on your new house is a great way to let go of your old house. The easiest way to start is on the internet. Look at the area in which you will be relocating. Get a notebook and start your lists. You will want to compare neighborhoods, schools, commute, shopping, and mere convenience. Begin listing and making choices, crossing out eliminations. Do you want to live in a planned development? New or old? An established neighborhood? Countryside? Rural? Inner City? On a farm? Let's start googling!

Search for homes in the areas you prefer. Begin with a broad search. It's generally not a good idea to begin with too many specifics. Give yourself the opportunity to see what's out there. This will also help in your choices. Start with your favorite specifications and price range.

Finding a Realtor® can be fun, too. If a friend or co-worker has referred someone, start there. Speaking to listing agents can give you a feel for you may be looking for. Call and ask general questions. Conduct your own personal interview. Within a short period of time you will most likely feel a connection with one of them. You will want to get along with your agent, as well as feel comfortable with their knowledge level and ability. You are hiring; your real estate agent will be working for you. Most likely, you will need to hire an agent in the area you will be moving and hiring a different listing agent to sell yours.

Now that you are clearer on where you are going, perhaps you are a little more motivated. You have a better feeling about it because you have taken time to look at what is available in the area you will soon be living.

It is time to prepare your house for market. A good place to start is to acquaint yourself with the home sales near your home. Search online in the area that you live in now, for homes for sale. Look for homes that are similar to yours. These properties are your competition. Try to be as objective as you can. There is so much at our fingertips now with online home searches that it won't take long for you to connect with a local agent to sell your home. While interviewing, ask about their process, marketing strategy, etc. It's not just about the selling price or the commissions. Ask them to perform an actual home audit, or a market analysis. This helps you see your own house as someone else may see it. You may consider purchasing your own home inspection. Your own home inspection helps you understand more about what you are selling, and can show you small ways to increase your home's value.

Now we're getting somewhere. There are lots of lists in your notebook and you need to try and make sense of them. So complete your interviewing and hire your listing agent. It is time to take pictures.

OH NO! PICTURES!?! Yes, there must be pictures. Too hard! Don't know how. Everything is a mess!

Remember all that searching you have been doing ? How did you limit your choices? You were looking at the pictures. Consider those that really stood out. Were they neat? Uncluttered? Trimmed landscapes? Fear Not! Not everyone lives like that.

You don't sell your home the way you live in your home, in general. These are two completely different things. It's called staging; and for the most part, this is some applied common sense. Start with your master bedroom and bath because it is the hardest.

Ready? Stand in your doorway and look at your bedroom. What do you see? OK, pick up the clothes and get the laundry done, now what do you see? Do you see the personal things you use every day? Do you see the little things that sit there because they're cute?

Do you see things like candles, a change tray, a jewelry box, lotions, perfumes?

Get a box or container, medium or small and place everything that you do not use every day that is personal in that box. Choose a few decorative items to leave in the room like a bedside lamp. Keep your bed made and your laundry down. Try to make your surfaces uncluttered.

Next prepare the kitchen. Basically, try to clear your countertops from all the small appliances and containers. Leave just a few on the countertops. Your dining table will look better with a central accent or decorative place settings.

Open the entry into your family area, living room by removing remove a sofa, love seat, or slide these big pieces to a linear position to give an open inviting atmosphere.

If you begin to feel overwhelmed, ask a friend to come over and enjoy the fun. It helps with the objectivity. And it's a good way to spend time with friends you will not see as often. Throughout your house, try not to have too many, if any, personal pictures and items around.

Remove prescription drugs from bathrooms and put them in a place where the visitors cannot find them. A bathroom is the only room in the house a real estate agent cannot be with their client. Put your valuables in your safe deposit box. It is only for a short while, and it is better to be safe about it.

What about your yard? Curb appeal is important, but your house does not have to be a million-dollar manicured landscape. Just clean it, trim it and perhaps add a little color of the season blooming.

Now, how's that list going for new houses? Don't wear yourself out over any one task. Try to take one step at a time. Or, I actually say, take one side step at a time. Step side to side and work on the new search, and then work on preparing your house to sell.

Even if you are not a seamstress, or cannot imagine

colors together or decorative themes and schemes, you probably have friends who do. You may want to incorporate their talents as you get your house ready to be shown. Or you can hire a professional.

There are professional stagers that will help you get your home ready to be viewed. They are a great asset; some real estate professionals are very gifted in that area. Staging includes common-sense de-cluttering. You are going to move anyway, so go ahead and pack up what you do not use every day. Perhaps you have an extra room, garage or utility space where you can begin storing your moving boxes.

That idea about new appliances really sounded good! Consider this: leave your appliances with your house. Leave your refrigerator and washer and dryer. That may be a great incentive for someone to buy, plus you get new ones! Begin thinking in those terms. For instance, say you have a large lawn to mow and where you are moving it will be small – consider leaving that big mower. Chances are the new buyers will not have one and it is a great incentive.

When you desire to sell your home for top dollar, and in your time frame, you need to do two things:

• Get control of your personal emotions about your home.

• Place yourself in the shoes of potential buyers. Look at your home the way they would, and make it appealing in the right areas.

I know that putting your "homeowner emotions" aside may be tough to do. But doing so will help you to position your home to sell, and in your time frame.

So it is no surprise that selling your home may involve a bit of sadness, fear or even excitement for the next move in your life.

After all, selling your home is very different from any other financial transaction. Your house is not just a *"thing."* It is where you have made your HOME! Try not to let these emotions get in the way of a prudent sale. So get a grip, get excited, and sell your house. You can do this!

ABOUT THE AUTHORS – *Lisa Jordan Watts, Phd,ThD*

Lisa Jordan Watts, PhD, ThD, is a North Carolina native. Lisa had a successful career as Minister of Music and Family Life Counselor for 23 years. She earned her undergraduate degree in France at the Universal Academy of Music along with her first M.A. in Performing Arts and continued her doctoral studies in Sacred Musicology. She completed two Masters degrees and her doctorate in Theological studies at Princeton Theological and Princeton University.

After a full career, Lisa settled down with her family and served her community in West Stanly County. Entrusted with the facilitating and development of the western office for the Stanly County Chamber of Commerce, she expanded her direction and focus to serve as an active liaison with the local merchants.

In January of 2011 Lisa sought her NC Real Estate Brokerage license. True to form, she hit the ground running and is now expanding the Classic Enterprises of Locust real estate division. Lisa Watts is an exclusive Service For Life!® Realtor®.

Contact Lisa Watts:

704-239-3872

www.lisawattshomes.com

www.lisawattshomes.blogspot.com

CPSIA information can be obtained at www.ICGtesting.com
Printed in the USA
BVOW080037240812

298583BV00002B/2/P